Frosted

TAKE YOUR BAKED GOODS TO THE NEXT LEVEL WITH
DECADENT BUTTERCREAMS, MERINGUES, GANACHES AND MORE

BERNICE BARAN, founder of Baran Bakery

PAGE STREET
PUBLISHING CO.

PAGE STREET
PUBLISHING CO.

First published in 2021 by
Page Street Publishing Co.
27 Congress Street, Suite 105
Salem, MA 01970
www.pagestreetpublishing.com

Distributed by Macmillan, sales in Canada by The Canadian Manda Group.

25 24 23 22 21   1 2 3 4 5

ISBN-13: 978-1-64567-294-4
ISBN-10: 1-64567-294-8

Library of Congress Control Number: 2020948802

Cover and book design by Laura Benton for Page Street Publishing Co.
Photography by Bernice Baran

Printed and bound in China

TO MY FAMILY, WHO INSPIRED IT,
BUT WILL PROBABLY NEVER READ IT.

Contents

INTRODUCTION

Welcome to *Frosted*, my friends, I'm so glad you're here! I think it's safe to assume that you're a fellow frosting lover, and you're here to literally put the icing on the cake . . . or cupcakes, cookies, donuts and pies! If you are like me, you believe that to elevate any recipe, you frost it.

Growing up, I always had a major sweet tooth. Having a mom as a baker only encouraged my baking habits. But it wasn't until I graduated college and started my nursing career that I actually learned how to bake. I started baking and posting on my blog, Baran Bakery, as a creative outlet on my off days, but I quickly realized that I wanted to do it every day. Learning about the science of baking drove me, it got me through my shifts and made me work harder and smarter to make that dream of baking full-time my reality.

I spent every free second learning about all things baking: what makes cakes grow, how to make cupcakes dome perfectly, why there are so many types of buttercream, why a frosting recipe isn't coming out correctly, how to salvage a broken buttercream and so much more. I wanted to know everything and, over the last few years, I've learned more than I could even imagine existed in the baking world. My blog went from a hobby to a business that I love: I teach others all I've learned and, hopefully, share my love of baking—and eating!—desserts. There are many ways to put a smile on people's faces, but serving a delicately frosted homemade dessert has got to be one of the best.

Frosting is a topic that can be intimidating, because there are so many types to learn about, each with its specific rules and challenges. Some frostings are similar and can be used interchangeably, but some are completely unique and only work under certain conditions. For example, a frosting like Diplomat Cream (page 23) needs to be refrigerated and can't sit out at room temperature for long, whereas most of the buttercreams can sit out for long periods of time.

Fueled by my curiosity and a desire to learn how to successfully make and use the most popular kinds of frostings, I experimented with each kind. In the process, I discovered the nuances of whipping up buttercreams, meringues, ganaches, creams and cream cheese frostings.

With this book, I'm happy to share all I've learned about these magical combinations of butter and sugar and to make you more confident with putting the icing on the cake!

HOW TO USE THIS BOOK

Frosted contains 60 recipes for baked goods, all of which use one of my thirteen frosting recipes. This means that there will be at least two parts to every recipe. Whether it's a cake, cookie, tart or bar, there will be a main recipe and one for frosting. Guys, there's a three-layer brownie cake frosted with caramel and a dark chocolate ganache frosting (page 31). There are peach donut shortcakes sandwiched around the fluffiest white chocolate buttercream filling (page 155). Don't even get me started on the Cookie Mocha Tart (page 178)! Think chocolate chip cookie crust, dark chocolate ganache filling and a toasted espresso meringue frosting: it's quite literally a frosted cookie coffee heaven.

Before you get started making these incredible desserts, it's important to learn the basics of each of the thirteen types of frosting that I include in the book. They are:

- American Buttercream (page 11)
- American Meringue Buttercream (page 12)
- Swiss Meringue Buttercream (page 13)
- Italian Meringue Buttercream (page 14)
- French Buttercream (page 15)
- German Buttercream (page 16)
- Ermine Buttercream (page 17)
- Russian Buttercream (page 18)
- Cream Cheese Frosting (page 19)
- Meringue Frosting (page 20)
- Chocolate Ganache (page 21)
- Bavarian Cream (page 22)
- Diplomat Cream (page 23)

For each frosting, I've included a breakdown of the flavor, texture and characteristics of that frosting, what it is best used for, which desserts it goes best with and a base recipe.

The base frosting recipes are what I find to be the simplest, most stable versions. They're delicious as is, and I left them unflavored so that they're easily customized to individual recipes. If, in your later baking, you ever need a basic frosting recipe, you can refer to this section and flavor it to your desire. Be sure to read through each frosting description and refer to some of my recipes when customizing your own.

As a part of each baked good recipe, you will see a reference to which base frosting it uses. I also tell you how to customize the base frosting to enhance the recipe. For example, for my Cookie Butter Chocolate Cake (page 37), you'll make a basic German Buttercream (page 16), to which you'll add vanilla bean paste and cookie butter.

When a dessert recipe calls for a double or triple batch of a base frosting, you can prepare the batches all together.

Many of the frostings are interchangeable in my recipes. For example, almost any buttercream frosting can be swapped out for another type of buttercream. I suggest how to swap in other frostings throughout the book as well.

I use a stand mixer for most of my recipes, but if you don't have one, fear not. You can use an electric hand mixer instead, just keep in mind that it will require more time and patience. I include time recommendations and visual cues in my recipe directions. If you're using a hand mixer to mix batters and frostings, make sure to refer more to the visual cues as opposed to the time suggestions.

I provide standard and metric measurements for all of the ingredients. Keep in mind that it's very easy to overmeasure dry ingredients, such as flour, cocoa powder and powdered sugar. Instead of scooping a cup of flour, spoon and level it. Use a spoon to fluff up the flour, then spoon the flour into the measuring cup. Allow it to overflow a little, then use the back of a knife to level off the flour.

TIP: MELTING CHOCOLATE

I'm all about chocolate of all kinds—dark, milk and white—and you'll find it used in many recipes in this book. I'm also all about convenience and ease, so I melt my chocolate in the microwave and give you instructions for doing so in my recipes.

An alternative is to use a double boiler. Bring ½ cup (120 ml) of water to a simmer in the bottom of a double boiler over medium-low heat. Add the chocolate to the top of the double boiler and cook it for about 5 minutes, stirring, until the mixture is smooth. For most recipes, you'll need to remove the melted chocolate from the heat to cool it to room temperature.

FROSTING 101

AMERICAN BUTTERCREAM

American Buttercream is one of the simplest frostings to make and possibly the most popular. It requires only an electric mixer, and both hand and stand mixers work well. This frosting is very sweet and doesn't require a lot of additives: just 1 to 2 teaspoons (5 to 10 ml) of extract goes a long way.

Depending on how American Buttercream is whipped, the texture can be light and fluffy or dense and thick. The longer it's whipped, the more air is incorporated, producing a fluffier frosting. Using a paddle attachment at low speed or pressing down on the buttercream with a rubber spatula will remove the excess air, making it easier to smooth this frosting over the outside of a layer cake. The consistency can easily be adjusted by adding more powdered sugar or more heavy whipping cream.

American Buttercream also dries out; it literally forms a crust when it's exposed to air. This can be really good for cake decorating—especially piping—because the buttercream will hold its shape really well. It's also easy to transport cakes frosted with American Buttercream because the edges are dried out. American Buttercream can be made with butter and/or shortening. Butter generally gives a better flavor, but does not do great in higher temperatures, such as at outdoor summer parties. Shortening has a more neutral flavor, but produces a more stable buttercream. I use butter in all of my recipes, but shortening can be substituted for the butter at a 1:1 ratio; many people like to use half butter and half shortening. The buttercream stays stable for a couple days at room temperature, a couple weeks in the refrigerator and a couple months in the freezer.

American Buttercream is very versatile. It is great for frosting cakes, cookies, brownies, cinnamon rolls, etc. Some of my favorites in the book include Double Chocolate Sugar Cookie Bars (page 129) and Butterscotch Banana Bread (page 151)! The sweetness and thick texture of American Buttercream are too much for more delicate desserts, such as sponge cakes. You'll find recipes using American Buttercream on pages 113, 129, 151 and 165.

YIELD: 2½ CUPS
(675 G)

1 cup (227 g) unsalted butter, room temperature

3½ cups (420 g) powdered sugar, spooned and leveled

2 tbsp (30 ml) heavy whipping cream, cold

⅛ tsp salt

Using a stand mixer fitted with a paddle attachment, beat the butter at medium-high speed for 1 to 2 minutes, until the color turns pale yellow. If you use shortening instead of butter, beat the shortening until it is smooth and fluffy.

Add the sugar to the butter and mix at low speed, just until combined. Turn the mixer back up to medium-high speed, and beat the buttercream for at least 5 minutes, until all of the sugar is fully dissolved and the buttercream no longer feels gritty. Make sure to scrape down the sides of the bowl with a rubber spatula as needed.

Pour in the cream and beat the mixture for 1 minute at medium-high speed. Add the salt and mix just until it's combined. If you want to remove the excess air to smoothly frost a cake, whip the buttercream on low speed for 3 to 5 minutes.

AMERICAN MERINGUE BUTTERCREAM

American Meringue Buttercream, also known as the lazy girl's Swiss Meringue Buttercream (page 13), combines the great Swiss Meringue Buttercream and American Buttercream in terms of flavor and method. I love this buttercream because it's the perfect balance between the buttery Swiss and supersweet American versions of buttercream. However, this frosting is not very fluffy, and the texture is pretty dense.

American Meringue Buttercream calls for a meringue, but my recipe uses pasteurized egg whites and powdered sugar, so we can skip the steps of cooking the egg whites and melting the sugar. This meringue is not going to get big or hold peaks: It's going to look more like a royal icing meringue.

American Meringue Buttercream is great for frosting cakes and piping; however, it does not form a crust when it's exposed to air. It can also be used for just about any type of dessert, such as Lemon Vanilla Bean Cake (page 57) or raspberry sugar cookies (page 109). Again, I would not pair it with something delicate, like a sponge cake, because of the dense texture. American Meringue Buttercream is used on pages 58, 109, 130 and 168.

YIELD: 2 CUPS
(524 G)

¼ cup (60 ml) pasteurized egg whites, room temperature

2 cups (240 g) powdered sugar, spooned and leveled

1 cup (227 g) unsalted butter, room temperature

⅛ tsp salt

Begin by thoroughly cleaning the aluminum bowl and the whisk attachment of the stand mixer; they can't have any fat residue when making meringue. Once they're clean and dry, whisk the egg whites and the sugar at medium-high speed for about 5 minutes, until the mixture is a little fluffy. It won't get big and fluffy like a Swiss or Italian meringue.

Add 1 to 2 tablespoons (14 to 28 g) of the butter at a time, beating on medium speed, until each chunk of butter is fully combined. Scrape down the sides of the bowl, turn the mixer up to high speed for a minute, then add the salt, mixing just until it's incorporated.

SWISS MERINGUE
BUTTERCREAM

Oh, the glorious Swiss Meringue Buttercream: It's the gateway to more than just American frosting. It's simple enough to make that most home bakers are willing to give it a try, but it's still incredibly luxurious. Like all of the European buttercreams, the Swiss version has a very buttery flavor and texture. It's so rich that I find it's quite difficult to flavor. For instance, you probably wouldn't notice if just 1 teaspoon of vanilla extract was added, whereas, in other frostings, 1 teaspoon is sufficient.

Swiss Meringue Buttercream is great to frost anything that will be served at room temperature or just slightly chilled. Because of the amount of butter in the recipe, the cream gets pretty firm when it's refrigerated. It is very smooth and fluffy at room temperature. Swiss Meringue Buttercream does not form a crust, but it does hold up well in heat. It is my go-to for all layer cakes and sheet cakes, because I love how silky and stable it is. You'll see that especially in my peanut butter chocolate sheet cake (page 85) and Banana Cookie Butter Cupcakes (page 98). Two other recipes (pages 63 and 93) also use Swiss Meringue Buttercream.

YIELD: 3 CUPS
(552 G)

4 large egg whites

1 cup (200 g) granulated sugar

1 cup (227 g) unsalted butter, room temperature

⅛ tsp salt

Begin by thoroughly cleaning a handheld whisk and the aluminum bowl and whisk attachment of the stand mixer; they can't have any fat residue when making meringue. Once they're clean and dry, place the egg whites and the sugar in the bowl.

In a small saucepan, bring ½ cup (120 ml) of water to a simmer. Keep the water simmering on low heat, and place the bowl with the egg whites and sugar on top of the saucepan, creating a double boiler. Using the handheld whisk, whisk the egg whites and sugar over low heat for 5 to 10 minutes, until the sugar granules are dissolved. The sugar is fully dissolved when you don't feel grains of sugar when you rub the mixture between your fingers. If you use a candy thermometer to test for doneness, bring the mixture to about 150°F (65°C).

Remove the bowl from the heat, place it on the stand mixer and beat the egg whites with the sugar at high speed, until stiff peaks form and the mixture is no longer warm. This usually takes 7 to 10 minutes. Lower the speed to medium, and slowly add the butter, 2 to 3 tablespoons (28 to 42 g) at a time. Once all of the butter is incorporated, continue beating the mixture on medium-high speed for a few minutes, or until it emulsifies into a buttercream. The mixture may go through phases of looking soupy and curdled before it emulsifies; if it doesn't emulsify after 5 to 10 minutes, see my Troubleshooting Guide (page 24). Scrape down the sides of the bowl, add the salt and mix just until it's incorporated.

ITALIAN MERINGUE
BUTTERCREAM

Italian Meringue Buttercream is very similar to Swiss Meringue Buttercream (page 13). The main difference is that the Italian version is known to be even more stable at higher temperatures, because it is made with a hot sugar syrup. Other than that, they share almost all of the same characteristics. Even the difference in taste is unnoticeable to most people: They're both pretty buttery. Italian Meringue Buttercream is smooth and fluffy at room temperature, but gets firm when it's refrigerated.

Italian Meringue Buttercream is lovely for layer cakes, sheet cakes, cupcakes, cookies and more. Be sure to try my brown butter version with the Brown Butter Birthday Cake (page 69). Three other recipes (pages 34, 97 and 114) use Italian Meringue Buttercream.

YIELD: 3 CUPS
(522 G)

3 egg whites

½ cup (100 g) + ¼ cup (50 g) granulated sugar, divided

3 tbsp (45 ml) water

1 cup (227 g) unsalted butter, room temperature

⅛ tsp salt

Begin by thoroughly cleaning the aluminum bowl and the whisk attachment of the stand mixer; they can't have any fat residue when making meringue. Once they're clean and dry, place the egg whites and ¼ cup (50 g) of the sugar in the bowl. Turn the mixer up to medium-high speed and beat the egg whites and sugar for 1 to 2 minutes, or until the meringue forms soft peaks.

Meanwhile, in a small saucepan over medium heat, cook the water and the remaining ½ cup (100 g) of sugar until it becomes a clear syrup and the temperature reaches 240°F (115°C); do not stir the mixture. Turn the mixer down to medium speed and, slowly, in a straight stream against the edge of the bowl, pour the hot sugar into the egg mixture. Turn the mixer up to high speed, and beat until the meringue is fully cooled and forms stiff peaks. This usually takes 7 to 10 minutes.

Lower the speed to medium and slowly add the butter, 2 to 3 tablespoons (28 to 42 g) at a time. Once all of the butter is incorporated, continue beating the mixture at high speed for a few minutes, or until it emulsifies into a buttercream. The mixture may go through phases of looking soupy and curdled before it emulsifies; if it doesn't emulsify after 5 to 10 minutes, see my Troubleshooting Guide (page 24). Scrape down the sides of the bowl, add the salt and mix just until it's incorporated.

FRENCH BUTTERCREAM

French Buttercream is thought to be the luxury of buttercreams. It's made in different ways, and many people use a combination of whole eggs and egg yolks. The first recipe I ever tried, by renowned French pastry chef Pierre Hermé, used egg yolks exclusively. I chose to stick with just egg yolks so that this buttercream tastes different from the Swiss (page 13) and Italian (page 14) Meringue Buttercreams.

Egg yolks generally lend a richer taste and color to baked goods and frostings, so French Buttercream has a little more flavor than the meringue buttercreams. It's significantly yellower in color, which can make it a little more difficult to reach desired colors for decorating. French Buttercream is very soft, smooth and silky. It is wonderful for creating that smooth finish on the outside of a cake; however, it does not hold up as well as meringue buttercream does in higher temperatures. French Buttercream can be used for decorating and piping, but it would not be my first choice because of the difficulty coloring it and how it reacts to heat. It's great for cakes, cupcakes, cookies and brownies/bars. A favorite recipe using French Buttercream is Dark Chocolate Marble Cake (page 47). Two other recipes (pages 71 and 117) also use French Buttercream.

YIELD: 3 CUPS
(564 G)

4 large egg yolks, room temperature

¼ cup (60 ml) water

1 cup (200 g) granulated sugar

1 cup (227 g) unsalted butter, room temperature

⅛ tsp salt

Place the egg yolks in the bowl of a stand mixer, and beat them on medium-high speed for 3 to 5 minutes, or until they are fluffy and pale yellow. Meanwhile, in a small saucepan over medium heat, cook the water and the sugar until it becomes a clear syrup and the temperature reaches 240°F (115°C); do not stir the mixture.

Turn the mixer down to medium speed and, slowly, in a straight stream against the edge of the bowl, pour the hot sugar into the egg yolks. Turn the mixer back up to high speed, and beat the mixture until it is fully cooled, 7 to 10 minutes.

Lower the mixer speed to medium, and slowly add the butter, 2 to 3 tablespoons (28 to 42 g) at a time. Once all of the butter is incorporated, continue beating on high speed for a few minutes until it emulsifies into a buttercream. The mixture may go through phases of looking soupy and curdled before it emulsifies; if it doesn't emulsify after 5 to 10 minutes, see my Troubleshooting Guide (page 24). Scrape down the sides of the bowl, add the salt and mix just until it's fully incorporated.

GERMAN BUTTERCREAM

German Buttercream was a pleasant surprise the first time I made it. Because German Buttercream uses an egg-based custard, it is thicker and not as fluffy a frosting as the other European buttercreams; it's more similar to the American Meringue Buttercream (page 12).

German Buttercream requires a similar amount of flavoring as the other European buttercreams. It colors easily and it also holds up great in heat, like the Italian Meringue Buttercream (page 14). German Buttercream is great for cakes, cupcakes, cookies and more. Some fun ones to try are the Cookie Butter Chocolate Cake (page 37) and the Oreo® Latte Cupcakes (page 89). Two other recipes (pages 79 and 148) use German Buttercream.

YIELD: 2½ CUPS (506 G)

½ cup (100 g) granulated sugar

2 tbsp (16 g) cornstarch

1 large egg

½ cup (120 ml) milk

1 cup (227 g) unsalted butter, room temperature

⅛ tsp salt

Whisk together the sugar and cornstarch in a small saucepan, then add the egg and milk, whisking until the mixture is fully combined. Place the saucepan over low heat, whisking the mixture continuously, until the custard has thickened enough to hold its shape, about 10 minutes. Remove the custard from the heat, and pour it into a heatproof bowl. Cover the surface with plastic wrap to prevent the custard from forming a skin, and allow the custard to cool completely at room temperature.

In the bowl of a stand mixer fitted with the whisk attachment, beat the butter and salt at medium-high speed, until the butter is pale in color, 2 to 3 minutes. Add the cooled custard to the butter in three to four increments, and continue beating the mixture until the buttercream is fluffy, about 5 minutes, making sure to scrape down the sides of the bowl as needed. Mix just until it's incorporated.

ERMINE BUTTERCREAM

Ermine Buttercream is like the Switzerland of frostings: totally neutral. She's an old-school buttercream that's not too sweet, not too buttery, not too heavy and not too light. My recipe differs a little from the standard, as I make a little less custard for the amount of butter used. My version is a little more stable at room temperature. There are many variables that affect the emulsification of buttercream. Heat is one of them, so I adapted this recipe so that it won't give you or me any problems, even in the middle of summer!

The best part about Ermine Buttercream is that, although it is really fluffy, it still holds up well with layer cakes. It wouldn't be my first choice for wedding cakes or piping, but it does hold up better than Cream Cheese Frosting (page 19). Like German Buttercream (page 16), Ermine Buttercream colors easily, but it may require more flavoring than American Buttercream (page 11).

It's fun to use Ermine Buttercream in Cookie Dough Brownie Bars (page 142) and White Chocolate Peach Donut Shortcakes (page 155). Other recipes (pages 55, 75, 90 and 161) also use Ermine Buttercream.

YIELD: 2½ CUPS
(577 G)

¾ cup (150 g) granulated sugar

¼ cup (30 g) all-purpose flour, spooned and leveled

¾ cup (180 ml) milk

1 cup (227 g) unsalted butter, room temperature

⅛ tsp salt

In a small saucepan, whisk together the sugar, flour and milk over medium-low heat. Whisk continuously, until the mixture coats the back of a spoon, about 5 minutes. Pour the mixture into a heatproof bowl, cover the surface with plastic wrap to prevent it from forming a skin and allow the custard to cool completely to room temperature.

In the bowl of a stand mixer, at medium-high speed, beat the butter and salt for about 5 minutes, until the butter is fluffy and pale. Slowly add the cooled custard, a little at a time, to the butter; adding the custard slowly prevents the mixture from clumping and the butter from deflating. When all of the custard is incorporated, scrape down the bowl, turn the mixer up to high speed and beat the buttercream for 1 minute. Mix just until it's incorporated.

RUSSIAN BUTTERCREAM

Russian Buttercream is just as simple as American Buttercream (page 11), if not simpler. It requires only three ingredients, but the process is specific. As with all of the buttercreams, the butter has to be at room temperature. But it also has to have sufficient air incorporated into it before adding the sweetened condensed milk. If the temperature is off just a little, or if there isn't enough air incorporated into the butter, the buttercream could easily split. There is an easy fix, though: just pop the buttercream into the fridge for half an hour, then whip it again. This frosting is best used right when it's made.

The sweetened condensed milk in Russian Buttercream gives it a sweet, creamy flavor. Like Cream Cheese Frosting (page 19), Russian Buttercream has a fluffy and silky texture. It is great for cakes, cupcakes and cookies. My favorite way to enjoy Russian Buttercream is to prepare it with dulce de leche, caramelized sweetened condensed milk, as in my churro cupcakes recipe (page 94). Three other recipes (pages 51, 141 and 152) use Russian Buttercream.

YIELD: 2½ CUPS
(425 G)

1 cup (227 g) unsalted butter, room temperature

7 oz (198 g) canned sweetened condensed milk, divided

⅛ tsp salt

Place the butter in the bowl of a stand mixer, and beat it at high speed for 5 to 10 minutes. You want the butter to look really pale and fluffy. Scrape down the sides of the bowl every couple of minutes.

Once the butter is pale and fluffy, turn the mixer speed down to medium, and slowly pour in half of the milk. When it's well incorporated, add the remaining half of the milk. Beat the mixture until the milk is fully combined, scraping down the sides of the bowl as needed. Add the salt, and mix just until it's well combined.

CREAM CHEESE FROSTING

Cream Cheese Frosting is a fan favorite, for sure! It's smooth, creamy and fluffy, not too buttery and the tang of the cream cheese balances the sweetness perfectly. It's hard to find someone who doesn't love Cream Cheese Frosting.

Essentially, it's the same as American Buttercream (page 11), except that it uses half butter and half cream cheese. Because cream cheese is much softer than butter, this frosting is going to be softer than any buttercream. Softer frosting is good for lightening up a heavy cake, frosting cinnamon rolls or filling pies. However, because it's so soft, Cream Cheese Frosting cannot stay at room temperature for long periods of time, so it would not be my first choice for frosting wedding cakes or piping decorations.

Cream Cheese Frosting is great with most types of desserts; carrot cake and cinnamon rolls are often paired with this frosting. It stars in my Pumpkin Marshmallow Cake (page 43) and Strawberries 'n' Cream Blondie Bars (page 133) and is used in several other recipes (pages 147, 157 and 174).

YIELD: 2½ CUPS (586 G)

½ cup (113 g) unsalted butter, room temperature

½ cup (113 g) cream cheese, room temperature

3 cups (360 g) powdered sugar, spooned and leveled

⅛ tsp salt

Use a stand mixer fitted with a paddle attachment to beat the butter and cream cheese at medium-high speed for 1 to 2 minutes, until the color turns into a pale yellow.

Add the powdered sugar to the butter mixture, and mix it at low speed, just until the sugar is combined, about 2 minutes. Turn the mixer to medium-high speed, and beat the frosting for at least 5 minutes, or until all of the sugar is fully dissolved and the frosting no longer feels gritty when pressed between your fingers. Scrape down the sides of the bowl as needed. Add the salt, and mix just until it's combined. If you want to remove excess air to more smoothly frost a cake, whip the frosting on low speed for an additional 3 to 5 minutes.

MERINGUE FROSTING

If I had to pick a favorite frosting, I would probably choose Meringue Frosting, which is also known as Seven-Minute Frosting. It's superlight and fluffy—kinda like homemade marshmallow fluff—complements just about everything and is superfun to torch. Meringue Frosting is not a buttercream, it is simply egg whites whipped with sugar to form a cloud of deliciousness.

This frosting is basically the first half of the Swiss (page 13) or Italian (page 14) Meringue Buttercream; you just don't add the butter or any fat. Because there is no butter, Meringue Frosting is incredibly soft and may not hold up well in a tall layer cake; however, it is great for cupcakes, sheet cakes, brownies, bars, pies and such.

If any fat is introduced to the meringue, it will break and become supersoft, so it can't be flavored with chocolate. You can add extracts and other fun things, such as powdered dried strawberries, which you'll find in my strawberry s'mores cookies (page 105) or espresso, as in the Cookie Mocha Tart (page 178). Meringue Frosting is also in several other recipes (pages 101, 106, 174, 182 and 185).

YIELD: 2 CUPS (160 G)

2 large egg whites
½ cup (100 g) granulated sugar
⅛ tsp salt

Begin by thoroughly cleaning a handheld whisk and the aluminum bowl and whisk attachment of the stand mixer; they can't have any fat residue when making meringue. Once the bowl is clean and dry, place the egg whites and the sugar in it.

In a small saucepan, bring ½ cup (120 ml) of water to a simmer. Keep the water simmering on low heat, and place the bowl with the egg whites and sugar on top of the saucepan, creating a double boiler. With the handheld whisk, whisk the egg whites and sugar over low heat for 5 to 10 minutes, until the sugar granules are dissolved. The sugar is fully dissolved when you don't feel grains of sugar when you rub the mixture between your fingers. If you use a candy thermometer to test for doneness, bring the mixture to about 150°F (65°C).

Remove the bowl from the heat, and place it in the stand mixer. Beat the mixture on medium-high speed, until stiff peaks form and the mixture is no longer warm. This usually takes 7 to 10 minutes. Add the salt, and mix again just until it's combined.

CHOCOLATE GANACHE

You'll notice that this book has a ton of recipes that use Chocolate Ganache, which is probably the most versatile dessert food on the planet. Make it with dark, milk or white chocolate, make it smooth and thick or make it whipped and creamy. There is no single description for Chocolate Ganache, because there are so many different variations, all depending on the ratio of chocolate to cream.

The directions are the same for each version. I included the ratios of chocolate to cream for a thin and thick version for dark chocolate, milk chocolate and white chocolate. You can experiment with different ratios to suit your taste.

Chocolate comes in so many forms and sizes that it is difficult to measure it precisely in measuring cups, so I recommend weighing it.

The thick Chocolate Ganache is great as a cake filling or for whipping into a frosting. The thin Chocolate Ganache is best for topping or drizzling. I love it on the Caramel Brownie Cake (page 31) and Millionaire Brownie Bars (page 123). Look for ganache in twelve more recipes (pages 40, 49, 65, 71, 101, 105, 110, 137, 138, 173, 178 and 182).

Place the chocolate in a heatproof bowl. Heat the cream in a small saucepan over low-medium heat until it's just simmering, not boiling, 1 to 2 minutes. Pour the hot cream over the chocolate, cover the bowl and let it stand for 1 to 2 minutes. Use a fork to slowly mix the chocolate, until it's smooth and fully incorporated with the cream. Use the chocolate ganache as directed in the recipe, either as-is or whipped.

To whip Chocolate Ganache, cover it and allow it to cool completely to room temperature. Once it's completely cool, use an electric mixer to whip it at high speed for 2 to 3 minutes, scraping down the sides of the bowl as needed. The color should lighten, and the chocolate frosting should hold stiff peaks. Add any extra flavors, and mix until they're fully incorporated.

YIELD: 1—2 CUPS
(185—312 G)

DARK CHOCOLATE GANACHE

THIN: 1:1 CHOCOLATE-TO-CREAM
6 oz (170 g) dark chocolate
¾ cup (180 ml) heavy whipping cream

THICK: 2:1 CHOCOLATE-TO-CREAM
6 oz (170 g) dark chocolate
⅜ cup (90 ml) heavy whipping cream

MILK CHOCOLATE GANACHE

THIN: 2:1 CHOCOLATE-TO-CREAM
6 oz (170 g) milk chocolate
⅜ cup (90 ml) heavy whipping cream

THICK: 3:1 CHOCOLATE-TO-CREAM
6 oz (170 g) milk chocolate
⅓ cup (80 ml) heavy whipping cream

WHITE CHOCOLATE GANACHE

THIN: 3:1 CHOCOLATE-TO-CREAM
6 oz (170 g) white chocolate
⅓ cup (80 ml) heavy whipping cream

THICK: 4:1 CHOCOLATE-TO-CREAM
6 oz (170 g) white chocolate
¼ cup (60 ml) heavy whipping cream

BAVARIAN CREAM

Bavarian Cream is interesting because it can actually just be a dessert on its own: no judgment if you eat this one with a spoon! I included it in my book because it was a type of frosting my mom used in her cakes when I was growing up. There are many different variations of Bavarian Cream; my recipe is pretty versatile.

For this recipe, I recommend a homemade stabilized whipped cream. You can also use Cool Whip®, which is a widely available store-bought whipped cream.

Desserts with this frosting can be served cold or at room temperature. To serve a dessert at room temperature, remove it from the refrigerator 30 minutes to 1 hour before serving.

Although Bavarian Cream contains gelatin and that keeps it stable enough for most baked goods, its base is still mostly whipped cream, so it may not be the best choice for tall layer cakes and decorating. It works with shorter cakes, donuts, pies and other treats. You'll see how I used Bavarian Cream with a cake in the Lemon Fruit Cake (page 81) and as a donut filling in the Chocolate Brioche Donuts (page 162). You'll find Bavarian Cream in two other recipes (pages 76 and 181).

YIELD: 6 CUPS
(1.34 KG)

BAVARIAN CREAM
6 large egg yolks

1 cup (200 g) granulated sugar

1½ cups (360 ml) milk

2 tsp (6 g) unflavored gelatin

⅛ tsp salt

STABILIZED WHIPPED CREAM (SEE TIP)
3 tbsp (45 ml) water, warm

2 tsp (6 g) unflavored gelatin

2½ cups (600 ml) heavy whipping cream, cold

½ cup (60 g) powdered sugar

For the Bavarian Cream, bring 1 cup (240 ml) of water to a simmer in a pot. Combine the egg yolks, sugar and milk in a large stainless steel bowl, and place it on top of the pot of water to create a double boiler. Whisk the ingredients frequently for a couple of minutes. When the mixture feels slightly warm, pour in the gelatin. Whisk continuously for about 10 minutes, until the mixture begins to thicken. It won't get quite as thick as custard, but it should coat the back of a spoon.

Remove the mixture from the heat, and continue to whisk it intermittently for just a few minutes. Then, cover the surface with plastic wrap to prevent it from forming a skin. Allow the mixture to cool just until it reaches room temperature. Do not refrigerate the mixture, as the gelatin will set.

When the custard is cooled, make the whipped cream. In a small bowl, combine the water and gelatin, and mix until the gelatin is dissolved. Set the bowl aside. Combine the cream and sugar in the bowl of a stand mixer, and use the whisk attachment to beat the mixture at medium speed until it thickens a bit, about 30 seconds. Turn the speed up to medium-high, and whisk the cream until soft peaks form, then pour in the gelatin. Continue to beat the whipped cream until it reaches stiff peaks, about 1 minute.

Add the cooled custard mixture to the whipped cream, and turn the mixer up to medium-high speed. Beat until the cream is fully combined, 1 to 2 minutes. Scrape down the sides of the bowl, add the salt and mix just until it's combined. The cream will still be quite soft at this point, but it will thicken on the cake after it's frosted.

TIP:
For convenience, you can use 16 ounces (454 g) of Cool Whip in place of the homemade stabilized cream.

DIPLOMAT CREAM

I would not be surprised if most of you have never heard of Diplomat Cream. It is very similar to Bavarian Cream (page 22), but there is no gelatin added to the custard. To make this a little more stable, the custard is made with butter instead of milk. Like Bavarian Cream, Diplomat Cream has many variations. This recipe from my mom is the one I grew up eating. It's obviously the best, so I didn't change a thing.

Just like the Bavarian Cream, Diplomat Cream requires a stabilized whipped cream.

Diplomat Cream can be used for just about any dessert, as long as it doesn't stay out at room temperature for too long. Desserts made with Diplomat Cream need to be stored in the refrigerator. Even though it's fairly soft, Diplomat Cream can be used for frosting layer cakes. If it gets too soft while you are frosting, refrigerate the cream and the cake until they harden a bit, then finish frosting. Keep in mind that some cakes are better served at room temperature, so they may not pair well with frostings that need refrigeration.

Two of my fan-favorite recipes use Diplomat Cream: the Tiramisu Brownies (page 134) and the Lemon Poppy Seed Blondie Pie (page 177). Two other recipes (pages 40 and 65) use this frosting as well.

YIELD: 3 CUPS (578 G)

DIPLOMAT CREAM
3 large egg yolks

¼ cup (50 g) granulated sugar

½ cup (113 g) unsalted butter, room temperature

⅛ tsp salt

STABILIZED WHIPPED CREAM (SEE TIP)
1 tbsp + 1 tsp (20 ml) water, warm

1 tsp unflavored gelatin

1¼ cups (300 ml) heavy whipping cream, cold

¼ cup (30 g) powdered sugar

Combine the egg yolks, sugar and butter in a medium saucepan. Whisk the mixture over medium-low heat continuously and quickly for about 10 minutes, until it begins to thicken into a custard. It should be thick enough to hold its shape for at least a few seconds.

Remove the custard from the heat and pour it into a heatproof bowl. Cover the surface with plastic wrap to prevent it from forming a skin, and allow the mixture to cool completely to room temperature.

When the custard is cooled, make the whipped cream. In a small bowl, combine the water and gelatin, and mix until the gelatin is dissolved. Set the bowl aside. Combine the cream and sugar in the bowl of a stand mixer, and use the whisk attachment to beat the mixture at medium speed until it thickens a bit, about 30 seconds. Turn the speed up to medium-high, and whisk the cream until soft peaks form; pour in the gelatin. Continue to beat the whipped cream until it reaches stiff peaks, 1 to 2 minutes.

Add the cooled egg mixture to the whipped cream, and turn the mixer up to medium-high speed. Beat until the cream is fully combined, 1 to 2 minutes. Scrape down the sides of the bowl, add the salt and mix just until it's combined. The cream will be superlight and fluffy.

TIP:
For convenience, you can use 8 ounces (227 g) of Cool Whip in place of the homemade stabilized cream.

TROUBLESHOOTING GUIDE

I could go to great lengths writing about troubleshooting frosting, because there are several ways--and whys—that things go wrong with frosting. Instead, I'll share my best tips and tricks to help you make your frosting recipes successful every time. To keep it short and sweet, I'll leave out the science behind some of the most common issues people encounter with frostings. I'll tell you when and how to save your frosting, so you'll always have the best frosting to top your dessert.

FLAVOR

Many people are disappointed to find that their frosting is either too sweet or too buttery. Keep in mind that, if you're making a buttercream recipe, the main ingredient is butter, and the frosting will taste like sweet butter. If you're making something like American Buttercream (page 11) or Cream Cheese Frosting (page 19), the main ingredient is powdered sugar, so the frosting will be very sweet.

To avoid a superbuttery frosting, I recommend adding strong flavors, like chocolate, coffee and peanut butter. I know vanilla is an American favorite, but sometimes it is just not a strong enough flavor to mask butter. I generally like to reserve my vanilla for recipes like Diplomat Cream (page 23), because it flavors easily and doesn't tolerate heavier additions, like jams, as well as the European buttercreams.

I also keep in mind that meringue-based buttercreams need more flavoring than the other buttercreams. For example, I add 1 teaspoon of vanilla extract to the American Buttercream (page 11), which uses 1 cup (227 g) of butter, but I would add 1 tablespoon (15 ml) to a Swiss Meringue Buttercream (page 13), which uses the same amount of butter. Of all of the buttercreams, the meringue-based buttercreams can absorb the most jam or preserves.

If you think a frosting, such as the American Buttercream (page 11) or Cream Cheese Frosting (page 19), is too sweet, reduce the amount of powdered sugar to your preference. Remember that the amount of sugar you add or remove can make your frosting softer or stiffer. Adding a little bit of salt or acid, like lemon juice, will help cut the sweetness as well. Also keep in mind that frosting tastes different on its own than it will when it's eaten with the dessert it is made for.

RUNNY BUTTERCREAM

Buttercream frosting can get runny, like soup, if the butter was too warm when it was added to a meringue-based buttercream frosting or if there is too much liquid in the frosting.

If you've used too-warm butter and the frosting is runny, refrigerate the buttercream for up to 30 minutes, then beat it again. The frosting is ready to beat again when the consistency changes from that of a runny soup to a thicker custard.

BEST FROSTING TEMPERATURE

Frosting is best to work with when butter is brought to room temperature in a kitchen that's between 68°F (20°C) and 73°F (23°C). In that temperature range, remove your butter from the fridge 1 to 2 hours before you plan to work with it. The butter is ready to use when it yields to pressure when you press it with your finger. If it looks greasy, it's too soft. If your kitchen is much cooler or much warmer than the range specified, add or subtract time from the 1- to 2-hour rule of thumb.

Liquid in buttercream comes from the egg whites, sugar and butter. My recipes specify large eggs; if you use extra-large eggs, the ratio of egg whites to butter will be off, and your buttercream won't emulsify. In this case, just add up to an extra ¼ to ½ cup (56 to 113 g) of butter. Add the butter a couple of tablespoons (28 g) at a time, every minute or so.

The same applies to sugar. Brown sugar holds more liquid than granulated sugar, so more butter is needed when brown sugar is used. You'll see this adjustment in my Peanut Butter Chocolate Cake (page 85). It calls for the Swiss Meringue Buttercream (page 13) to be made with the same amount of brown sugar as the granulated sugar in the base recipe. But for the peanut butter buttercream, you have to add an extra 2 to 3 tablespoons (28 to 42 g) of butter.

Generally, the brand of butter doesn't make a difference, though different brands of butter contain different amounts of fats and water. American butter can go as low as 80 percent butterfat, which is why some butters get saggy and greasy at room temperature, and European butter is generally 82 to 86 percent butterfat. Either of these can be used to make buttercream. Be sure to never use a butter spread, because they usually have less than 80 percent butterfat and contain additives.

CURDLED BUTTERCREAM

There are two main reasons why buttercream splits: the butter was too cold or there is too much liquid.

If your buttercream curdles or splits, it usually means the butter was too cold. This is very common with meringue-based buttercreams, but it can also happen with simple frostings like American Buttercream (page 11) or Cream Cheese Frosting (page 19). A frosting can also separate if it uses more than one fat and they are at different temperatures, such as when butter is room temperature but the cream cheese is cold. You want to have the butter soft enough so it yields when you press your finger into it with a little pressure, but not so soft that it looks greasy. Since my kitchen is a little warm, I usually leave my butter on the counter overnight. Then, when I put the egg whites and sugar over the double boiler, I'll pop the butter into the fridge for 10 minutes so it's not too soft.

There are three ways to fix curdled or split buttercream:

1. With the mixer running on medium speed, heat the outside of the bowl with a blow dryer to soften the buttercream; beat the mixture until it emulsifies again.

2. If you don't have a blow dryer, remove several spoonfuls of the buttercream, and microwave it in 10-second intervals until it's fully melted. Turn the mixer back up to medium speed, and pour in the melted buttercream. Then beat the mixture until it emulsifies.

3. You can also just place the whole bowl over a double boiler at low heat, hand-mix the buttercream until it warms up a little, then beat it again. If the buttercream turns soupy but it's no longer curdled, refrigerate it and then beat it again.

If your buttercream split only after adding an ingredient such as jam or preserves, then you either added too much or the specific type used contained too much liquid. In this case, I would add an extra ½ cup (113 g) of butter, then beat the buttercream at high speed; keep in mind that this will alter the flavor, making it more buttery. If this doesn't work, try warming up the buttercream using one of the above methods.

BROKEN GANACHE

Unfortunately, if your Chocolate Ganache (page 21) splits, it is quite difficult to salvage it. Chocolate has many reasons to split, including overheating and overmixing. My first recommendation is to reheat the chocolate over a double boiler while stirring it. You could also try adding a couple teaspoons of room temperature milk, not cream, or liquor. Something that usually works for me is making another batch of ganache and combining it with the broken one. However, if you don't have a use for the extra ganache, it may just be safer to toss the broken one and make a new one.

LUMPY OR GRAINY FROSTING

If any frosting with powdered sugar feels a little grainy, first try beating it at high speed for a few minutes. If that doesn't help, then try adding 1 tablespoon (15 ml) of cream and beating it again. If that also doesn't help, then it may be the type of sugar used; look for powdered sugar with added cornstarch.

If any of the custard-based frostings are lumpy, it's probably because, when the custard was cooked, some of the eggs coagulated. You can strain the custard while it's still warm and then proceed. Lumps can also be caused by cold custard. The custard should be at room temperature and not chilled before it's mixed with the whipped cream. You can try to remove the lumps by switching to the flat beater and beating the cream at high speed, but that might not get them all out. If they're larger chunks, just remove them with a fork; the frosting should still be edible, it just may not look very nice.

If any of the European buttercreams feel gritty, that is usually because the sugar was not fully dissolved in the beginning steps. This can happen because the mixture did not get hot enough or there was too much sugar for the amount of liquid. Causes also include measuring inaccurately or using eggs smaller than large, which contain less liquid. Unfortunately, I have not discovered a way to make the sugar dissolve once the butter is emulsified.

For the Italian Meringue (page 14) and French (page 15) Buttercreams, it is important to use a very clean saucepan for the syrup and not to touch the syrup at all when it's cooking. As with making caramel, if one sugar crystal is introduced in the syrup, it can crystallize the whole thing. It's also important, when you add the syrup to the mixer, to make sure the hot sugar syrup is running in a straight stream against the side of the bowl and not onto the moving whisk. If the syrup hits the whisk on the way down, it will splash, cooling it before it reaches the meringue and crystallizing.

AIR BUBBLES

Personally, I don't care about air bubbles, as I don't do much cake decorating. I prefer my frosting to have a lot of air, because it makes it feel lighter and it increases the volume a little. However, if you are having trouble frosting a cake because of the air bubbles, switch the mixer to a flat beater, and beat the frosting on low speed for 5 to 10 minutes. Then, use your rubber spatula to fold the frosting onto itself, pushing out some more of the air.

LUSCIOUS
LAYERS

Layer cakes are my absolute favorite thing to bake. Layer cakes are the best because, although they can be simple and basic, they can also be unique and customizable. I love combining different flavors and textures to turn classics into something more unique and fun. Take the Caramel Brownie Cake (page 31) for example. The flavors are nothing out of the ordinary; the cake has just brownies, caramel and ganache. But, have you ever seen three layers of brownies stuck together with homemade salted caramel and a dark chocolate ganache frosting? I didn't think so.

People are always impressed with layer cakes. They perform the best on my blog and social media accounts, even though they really don't taste much different from sheet cakes or cupcakes. Obviously, it's all those luscious-looking layers that make these sky-high cakes so attractive!

I know layer cakes can be intimidating, especially if you've never made one before. If it's your first time, my advice is to follow the recipe precisely, get comfortable with your cake and your buttercream, DON'T EVER skip refrigeration time if a recipe calls for it and read the Trimming & Frosting Layer Cakes section I've included for you below.

If I could bake only one thing for the rest of my life, it would absolutely be layer cakes, simply because they have so much variety. Other than when I have tested and retested recipes, I don't think I've ever baked the same cake twice.

TRIMMING & FROSTING LAYER CAKES

Making layer cakes takes time, but impressing people with your creations makes it worthwhile. The edges of a cake bake quicker than the centers, resulting in a domed cake. The domes, if not trimmed, can make a layer cake look awkward or make it unstable. Here are tips for trimming the domes of cakes, as well as the steps for layering, filling and frosting cakes.

1. FIRMING: Once the cakes have cooled at room temperature, wrap them tightly in plastic wrap and place them in the freezer for 1 to 2 hours or in the refrigerator overnight.

2. TRIMMING: I've found that 6-inch (15-cm) cakes don't usually dome because the cake is so small. Here is how to trim the tops of larger cakes:

You can eyeball the trim or use a ruler. If you have a turntable, it will be a little easier because it spins. Put the completely cooled cake on a turntable, cutting board or other flat service. Measure the shortest side of the cake. Use a knife to make four to five marks all around the cake at the height where it's shortest; you are putting the marks at the juncture of the flat part of the cake and the dome. Now, use a large, serrated knife to cut off the domed part of the cake, using the marks as a guide. Repeat this process for any remaining layers.

3. FROSTING LAYERS: Place the first layer of the cake on a flat surface—a turntable, cutting board, plate, cake stand or cake board all work. Use an offset spatula to frost the layer with the desired amount of frosting. I usually make it about ½ inch (1.3 cm) thick, depending on the recipe. Stack the next layer of cake on top, and repeat for the remaining layers.

4. FILLING LAYERS: If you want to fill your cakes with something other than a stable buttercream, such as curd or pastry cream, fill a piping bag with buttercream and pipe a thick border right at the edge of the cake. Then, fill the middle with your filling and repeat for all of the layers. If any cream squeezes out between the layers, smooth it gently with an offset spatula. Now, refrigerate the cake for at least 30 minutes, until the cake feels firm.

5. APPLYING A CRUMB COAT: Remove the cake from the fridge, and frost the outside of the cake with a *crumb coat*. This is a thin layer of frosting that ensures all the crumbs get caught and don't end up showing in your final coat of frosting. Then, refrigerate the cake again for at least 30 minutes.

6. FROSTING: Place the rest of the buttercream on top of the cake, and use an offset spatula to work the buttercream evenly across the top and down the sides, until the cake is fully covered

7. SMOOTHING: Gently place a cake scraper against the edge of the cake. Spin the turntable, and keep the cake scraper at about a 45-degree angle, so the frosting is getting scraped onto the cake and not wiped off. If you don't have a turntable to spin the cake, just move a little slower and gently turn the cake with your free hand. Some of the frosting should have created uneven ridges at the top of the cake. Leave those there, and refrigerate the cake for 30 to 60 minutes.

8. EDGING: Remove the cake from the fridge, and run the offset spatula under very hot water. Use the hot spatula to gently slice off the frosting at the top, creating a perfect edge. Proceed to decorating the cake as desired.

CAKE-FROSTING TIP
Make sure your buttercream is at a good temperature and consistency when you frost a cake. You want it soft enough to spread, but not so soft that when you place another cake layer on top, all the frosting squeezes out. If at any point the frosting feels too soft and the cake is unsteady, refrigerate the frosting for 20 minutes, or until it firms up a little.

CARAMEL BROWNIE CAKE

I mean is there a better way to start a book than with gooey layers of brownie slapped together with creamy caramel and Dark Chocolate Ganache (page 21)? I didn't think so either. Making a brownie cake was on my to-do list for at least a year, and this cake is one of the recipes I was most excited about when I planned which recipes to include in this book. This cake is rich and indulgent, unique but familiar and certainly impressive.

For the brownie, grease three 8 x 8–inch (20 x 20–cm) baking pans with baking spray, then line the pans with parchment paper, leaving an overhang of paper above the tops of the pans to easily remove the brownies. Preheat the oven to 325°F (163°C).

In a small bowl, melt the butter, canola oil and the chocolate chips for 20-second intervals in the microwave, stirring after each interval, until the mixture is smooth, 1 to 2 minutes. Set aside the mixture to cool for a minute.

In a small bowl, whisk together the flour, cocoa powder and salt until they're evenly distributed.

In a large bowl, whisk together the eggs, granulated and brown sugars until they're just barely combined. Don't overmix. Whisk the chocolate mixture into the egg mixture, then sift the dry ingredients over the wet, mixing just until the last streak of flour is combined.

Distribute the batter evenly among the prepared pans. Bake the brownies for about 35 minutes, until the centers look set. Remove the brownies from the oven, and allow them to cool, in the pans, to room temperature.

For the caramel sauce, place the sugar and water in a medium, light-colored saucepan with a lid over medium heat. Allow the sugar to melt in the water but DO NOT STIR IT. After about 10 minutes, when the color of the sugar begins to turn amber, remove the pan from the stove and stir in the cream. The mixture will bubble violently, so be careful. Stir the mixture until the cream is completely combined, whisk in the butter and pour the caramel into a heatproof bowl. Add the vanilla and salt, mixing until they're completely combined. Cover the caramel and allow it to cool to room temperature before refrigerating it.

(Continued)

BROWNIE
1 cup (227 g) unsalted butter, softened

½ cup (120 ml) canola oil

2 cups (350 g) semisweet chocolate chips

2¼ cups (270 g) all-purpose flour, spooned and leveled

½ cup (40 g) Dutch-process cocoa powder, spooned and leveled

1 tsp salt

8 large eggs, room temperature

2 cups (400 g) granulated sugar

1 cup (190 g) packed brown sugar

CARAMEL SAUCE
1 cup (200 g) granulated sugar

¼ cup (60 ml) water

½ cup (120 ml) heavy whipping cream, room temperature

½ cup (113 g) unsalted butter, softened

½ tsp vanilla extract

½ tsp salt

Make the three batches of the Thick Dark Chocolate Ganache.

Use the overhanging parchment paper to lift the brownie layers from the pans. Put the first brownie layer on a flat surface, then use a piping bag to pipe a border of ganache on it. Fill in the border with a layer of caramel, as much as you can without it spilling out, and then refrigerate the cake layer for 20 minutes. Repeat with the second layer of brownie and caramel, reserving a bit of the caramel for the top of the cake. Place the third layer on top, and refrigerate the cake for at least 1 hour, until the ganache feels firm and the cake feels stable. Then, frost the top of the cake with the rest of the ganache and drizzle the ganache with caramel.

This Caramel Brownie Cake is best served slightly chilled. Store it in an airtight container in the fridge for up to a week.

WHIPPED CHOCOLATE GANACHE FROSTING
3 batches of Thick Dark Chocolate Ganache (page 21)

FROSTED ANIMAL CRACKER CAKE

I'm pretty sure this Frosted Animal Cracker Cake is what dreams are made of. At least my dreams. Admit it: bits of frosted animal crackers in a vanilla cake, frosted with a supersilky white chocolate Italian Meringue Buttercream (page 14) is pretty hard not to dream about.

YIELD: 8—10 SLICES

CAKE

2¼ cups (270 g) all-purpose flour, spooned and leveled

2½ tsp (12 g) baking powder

½ tsp salt

¼ cup (60 g) unsalted butter, room temperature

½ cup (120 ml) canola oil

1½ cups (300 g) granulated sugar

3 large eggs, room temperature

¾ cup (170 g) sour cream

1 tsp vanilla extract

¾ cup (180 ml) milk, room temperature

1 cup (150 g) roughly chopped frosted animal crackers

For the cake, preheat the oven to 350°F (177°C). Grease three 6-inch (15-cm) cake pans with baking spray, and line them with parchment paper.

In a medium bowl, whisk together the flour, baking powder and salt.

In the bowl of a stand mixer fitted with the whisk attachment, beat the butter, oil and sugar on medium speed, until the mixture is light and fluffy. This should take 2 to 3 minutes. Then add the eggs, one at a time, beating well after each addition for about 30 seconds. Scrape down the sides and bottom of the bowl as needed. Add the sour cream and vanilla, and mix just until they're combined.

With the mixer at low speed, add half of the dry ingredients to the mixture, followed by the milk and then the second half of the dry ingredients. Increase the mixer speed to medium, and beat the mixture just until the flour is fully incorporated, making sure to scrape the flour from the sides of the bowl. Fold in the animal crackers, mixing until they're evenly distributed.

Distribute the batter evenly among the prepared pans, filling each pan only one-half to two-thirds full. Bake the cakes for about 40 minutes, until an indentation made with your finger in the top center of the cake springs back. If the indentation remains, return the cakes to the oven for 2 minutes, or until the center springs back. Remove the cakes from the pans, and allow them to cool completely before frosting them.

(Continued)

For the animal cracker buttercream, make a batch of Italian Meringue Buttercream. While the meringue is beating, melt the white chocolate chips in a small bowl in the microwave for 15-second intervals, stirring after each interval, until smooth, about 1 minute. After the butter is fully incorporated into the frosting, add the melted chocolate, vanilla bean paste and almond extract, mixing just until they're combined.

Place the first layer of cake on a flat surface and use an offset spatula with half of the frosting to frost the first and then the second layer of cake. Place the third layer on top, and then smooth any buttercream that squeezed out between the layers. Apply a thin crumb coat to the outside of the cake and refrigerate it for at least 30 minutes.

Divide the remaining buttercream in half, adding pink food coloring to one half. Then, divide the pink buttercream in half and make one-half a darker pink. Use an offset spatula to randomly apply the different shades of buttercream to the cake. When the colors look evenly dispersed on the cake, use a cake scraper to smooth the top and sides of the cake. Try not to work the buttercream too much, or the colors will all begin to blend and make the whole cake one color.

This Frosted Animal Cracker Cake is best served at room temperature or slightly chilled. Store it in an airtight container in the fridge for up to a week.

FROSTED ANIMAL CRACKER ITALIAN MERINGUE BUTTERCREAM

1 batch of Italian Meringue Buttercream (page 14)

½ cup (87 g) white chocolate chips

1 tsp vanilla bean paste or high-quality vanilla extract

½ tsp almond extract

Pink gel food coloring

COOKIE BUTTER CHOCOLATE CAKE

I don't even know what to say about this cake, because there are no words to describe it. I guess you can say I'm a bit of a cookie butter addict, so pairing cookie butter with chocolate cake and German Buttercream (page 16) is pure bliss. Family members who taste-tested this cake said, "If this is going in your book, it will be the No. 1 showstopper."

Begin by making the custard for the German Buttercream at least a few hours before frosting the cake, so it has time to cool.

To make the chocolate cake, preheat the oven to 350°F (177°C), grease three 6-inch (15-cm) cake pans with baking spray and line the pans with parchment paper.

In a medium bowl, whisk together the flour, sugar, cocoa powder, baking soda, baking powder, espresso powder and salt.

In a large bowl, whisk together the eggs, oil, buttermilk, coffee and vanilla until they're well combined. Sift the dry ingredients over the wet, and fold them together just until the last streak of flour is combined.

Distribute the batter evenly among the prepared cake pans, filling them only one-half to two-thirds full. Bake the cakes for 35 to 40 minutes, until an indentation made with your finger in the top center of the cake springs back. If the indentation remains, return the cakes to the oven for 2 minutes, or until the center springs back. Remove the cakes from the pans, and allow them to cool completely before frosting.

Finish the German Buttercream, then add the vanilla bean paste and the cookie butter, and mix just until they're fully incorporated.

(Continued)

YIELD: 8–10 SLICES

COOKIE BUTTER GERMAN BUTTERCREAM

1 batch of German Buttercream (page 16)

1 tsp vanilla bean paste or high-quality vanilla extract

¾ cup (180 g) cookie butter (I use Lotus Biscoff)

CHOCOLATE CAKE

2 cups (240 g) all-purpose flour, spooned and leveled

2 cups (400 g) granulated sugar

1 cup (80 g) Dutch-process cocoa powder, spooned and leveled

½ tsp baking soda

1 tsp baking powder

1 tsp espresso powder

½ tsp salt

2 large eggs, room temperature

¾ cup (180 ml) canola oil

¾ cup (180 ml) buttermilk, room temperature

¾ cup (180 ml) brewed coffee, room temperature

1 tsp vanilla extract

LUSCIOUS LAYERS

39

COOKIE BUTTER CHOCOLATE CAKE
(Continued)

For the topping, place the cookie butter in a heatproof bowl. Microwave it for 10 to 15 seconds, until it's thin enough to drizzle.

Place the first layer of cake on a flat surface, and spread it with one-quarter of the buttercream. Top the buttercream with half of the speculoos cookies, and drizzle on one-third of the cookie butter. Repeat with the second layer of cake and then place the third layer on top. Smooth out any buttercream that squeezed out between the layers, and refrigerate the cake for at least 30 minutes.

Frost the cake with a thin layer of buttercream as the crumb coat, and refrigerate the cake for 30 minutes. Place the remaining buttercream on top of the cake. Use an offset spatula to work the buttercream down the sides, and use a cake scraper to smooth it all out. Refrigerate the cake until the outer layer is set, about 30 minutes.

Reheat the remaining one-third of the cookie butter, then drizzle it on top of the cake. Refrigerate the cake for a few minutes, until the cookie butter sets.

This Cookie Butter Chocolate Cake is best served at room temperature. Store it in an airtight container in the fridge for up to a week.

TOPPING
¾ cup (180 g) cookie butter (I use Lotus Biscoff)

5 speculoos cookies (I use Lotus Biscoff), crushed into pea-sized chunks, divided

HUNGARIAN DOBOS TORTE

This one's for all of my Romanian friends! If you've ever tried my mom's Dobos torte and you wanted the recipe, your dreams have come true! This is more than just a classic vanilla sponge cake with chocolate frosting. It's 10 layers of pillowy soft vanilla sponge cake, frosted with clouds of chocolate Diplomat Cream (page 23) and covered in a rich Dark Chocolate Ganache (page 21) that epitomizes a chocolate frosting lover's dream.

Begin by making the custard for the batches of Diplomat Cream at least a few hours before frosting the cake, so it has time to cool. Then, finish making the rest of the cream and stir in the melted chocolate chips, vanilla bean paste and cocoa powder. Beat the mixture on medium-high speed until it's fully combined, making sure to scrape down the sides of the bowl as needed. Set aside the cream while you bake the sponge.

For the sponge cake, arrange racks at the top and middle of the oven, and preheat it to 350°F (177°C). Grease two 18 x 13–inch (46 x 33–cm) baking sheets with baking spray.

Place the egg whites in a large bowl with the water. Use an electric mixer to beat the egg whites on high speed for 30 to 60 seconds, until they begin to look frothy. Add the sugar and beat the mixture on high speed for 1 to 2 minutes, until it is really fluffy. Lower the speed to medium and add the egg yolks and oil, mixing until they're fully combined. Reduce the speed to low, and sift half of the flour in and mix just until it's almost incorporated. Repeat with the remaining flour, making sure to scrape down the sides of the bowl. Don't overmix; you want the batter to be light and very fluffy.

Use an offset spatula to spread a thin layer of batter on each of the prepared pans; be sure to make the batter flat and smooth. You want the layer to be as thin as possible without being able to see through to the baking sheet. Bake the layers on the top and middle racks of the oven for 5 to 7 minutes, until they're golden brown. Remove the pans from the oven, flip them over, as if you're removing a cake from a regular baking pan, and use a large knife to release each sheet from the pan. Repeat until the batter is finished to make 5 full sheets of layers; regrease the pans between baking the layers.

(Continued)

CHOCOLATE DIPLOMAT CREAM
2 batches of Diplomat Cream (page 23)

½ cup (87 g) dark chocolate chips, melted and cooled

1 tsp vanilla bean paste or high-quality vanilla extract

¼ cup (20 g) cocoa powder, spooned and leveled

VANILLA SPONGE
6 large eggs, separated and room temperature, divided

2 tbsp (30 ml) water

½ cup (100 g) granulated sugar

½ cup (120 ml) canola oil

1 cup (120 g) all-purpose flour, spooned and leveled

The sheets cool very quickly, so once you put the second round in the oven, you can begin putting the cake together. Cut each sheet in half lengthwise, place one half on a flat surface and begin frosting. Frost with a layer of the Chocolate Diplomat Cream about as thin as the sheet itself. Repeat until you have 10 total layers of cake and 10 layers of cream. Refrigerate the cake for 2 to 3 hours, until the cream feels set.

Once the cream is firm, use a large, serrated knife to trim the edges of the cake, making it all even. Place the remaining Chocolate Diplomat Cream on top, and use an offset spatula to work it down around the edges of the cake. Use a cake scraper to smooth the edges, and then refrigerate the cake for at least 1 hour, until the cream is set again.

Make the ganache and pour it over the chilled cake. Refrigerate the cake for a couple of hours to let the ganache set.

This Hungarian Dobos Torte is best served slightly chilled. Store it in an airtight container in the fridge for up to a week.

CHOCOLATE GANACHE
1 batch of Thin Dark Chocolate Ganache (page 21)

PUMPKIN MARSHMALLOW CAKE

I LOVE baking with pumpkin. In fact, it's one of the reasons I became a baker. I always loved fall flavors, and baking with pumpkin was one of my first challenges. The only thing that could make pumpkin cake better is a chai-spiced caramel sauce and a Toasted Marshmallow Cream Cheese Frosting. Yeah, you read that right, I add warm toasted marshmallows to Cream Cheese Frosting (page 19)!

For the caramel sauce, place the sugar and water in a medium, light-colored saucepan with a lid over medium heat. Allow the sugar to melt in the water, but DO NOT STIR IT. After about 10 minutes, when the sugar begins to turn an amber color, remove the pan from the stove and stir in the cream. The mixture will bubble violently, so be careful. Stir the mixture until it's completely combined, whisk in the butter and pour the caramel into a heatproof bowl. Add the vanilla, salt, cinnamon, ginger, cloves, nutmeg, cardamom and pepper, mixing until they're completely combined. Cover the caramel and allow it to cool to room temperature.

For the cake, preheat the oven to 350°F (177°C). Grease three 6-inch (15-cm) cake pans with baking spray, and line them with parchment paper.

In a medium bowl, whisk together the flour, baking soda, baking powder, salt, cinnamon, nutmeg, cloves, ginger, cardamom and pepper.

In a large bowl, whisk together the eggs, granulated and brown sugars, oil, pumpkin and vanilla, until the mixture is completely smooth. Add the dry ingredients to the wet ingredients, and whisk just until the last streak of flour is combined. Distribute the batter evenly among the prepared pans, filling each pan only about one-half to two-thirds full.

Bake the cakes for about 35 minutes, until an indentation made with your finger in the top center of the cake springs back. If the indentation remains, return the cakes to the oven for 2 minutes, or until the center springs back. Remove the cakes from the pans, and allow them to cool completely before frosting.

(Continued)

CHAI-SPICED CARAMEL SAUCE

½ cup (100 g) granulated sugar

2 tbsp (30 ml) water

¼ cup (60 ml) heavy whipping cream, room temperature

2 tbsp (28 g) unsalted butter, softened

½ tsp vanilla

¼ tsp salt

¼ tsp cinnamon

⅛ tsp ginger

⅛ tsp cloves

⅛ tsp nutmeg

⅛ tsp cardamom

Pinch of black pepper

CHAI SPICE PUMPKIN CAKE

3 cups (360 g) all-purpose flour, spooned and leveled

1 tsp baking soda

2 tsp (10 g) baking powder

½ tsp salt

2 tsp (4 g) cinnamon

1 tsp nutmeg

1 tsp cloves

1 tsp ginger

1 tsp cardamom

¼ tsp black pepper

4 large eggs, room temperature

1 cup (200 g) granulated sugar

PUMPKIN MARSHMALLOW CAKE *(Continued)*

For the Toasted Marshmallow Cream Cheese Frosting, preheat the oven to 400°F (205°C), and line a baking sheet with parchment paper. Make the batch of Cream Cheese Frosting.

Place the marshmallows on the prepared baking sheet, and bake them for about 5 minutes. Stand next to the oven and watch the marshmallows toast; as soon as they brown, remove them from the oven and scrape them into the bowl of Cream Cheese Frosting. Add the vanilla bean paste. Beat the frosting, at medium-high speed, just until the marshmallows are fully combined. Refrigerate the frosting for 30 minutes. Remove the frosting from the fridge, and mix it with a spatula to smooth it out a bit.

Place the first layer of cake on a flat surface and use an offset spatula with half of the frosting to frost the first and then the second layer of cake. Place the third layer on top, then smooth out any frosting that squeezed out between the layers.

Apply a thin crumb coat to the outside of the cake, and refrigerate the cake for at least 1 hour.

Place the rest of the frosting on top of the cake and, with the offset spatula, work it down the sides. Use the offset spatula or a cake scraper to smooth out the top and sides of the cake as needed. Refrigerate the cake for at least 30 minutes before drizzling the caramel on top.

This Pumpkin Marshmallow Cake is best served at room temperature or slightly chilled. Store it in an airtight container in the fridge for up to a week.

CHAI SPICE PUMPKIN CAKE (CONTINUED)

1 cup (190 g) packed brown sugar

1 cup (240 ml) canola oil

1 (15-oz [425-g]) can pumpkin puree

1 tsp vanilla extract

TOASTED MARSHMALLOW CREAM CHEESE FROSTING

1 batch of Cream Cheese Frosting (page 19)

10 large marshmallows

1 tsp vanilla bean paste or high-quality vanilla extract

BLUEBERRY CARDAMOM CAKE

This cake happened by accident. I wanted to test a strawberry Swiss Meringue Buttercream (page 13), but then realized I had only blueberry preserves. So, I had a delicious blueberry buttercream with no cake. Cinnamon-flavored inspiration struck, and I was shocked at how well the blueberry buttercream paired with my new cardamom cinnamon cake. It's the perfect combination of warm spices and fresh fruit!

For the cake, preheat the oven to 350°F (177°C). Grease three 6-inch (15-cm) cake pans, and line them with parchment paper. In a medium bowl, whisk together the flour, baking powder, salt, cardamom and cinnamon.

In the bowl of an electric mixer fitted with the whisk attachment, beat the butter, oil and granulated and brown sugars, on medium speed, until they're light and fluffy. This should take 2 to 3 minutes. Then add the eggs, one at a time, beating well after each addition for about 30 seconds. Make sure to scrape the sides and bottom of the bowl as needed. Add the sour cream and vanilla, and mix just until they're combined.

With the mixer at low speed, add half of the dry ingredients to the mixture, followed by the milk and then the second half of the dry ingredients. Increase the mixer speed to medium, and beat the mixture, just until the flour is fully incorporated, making sure to scrape the flour from the sides of the bowl.

Distribute the batter evenly among the prepared pans, filling each pan only one-half to two-thirds full. Bake for about 35 minutes, until an indentation made with your finger in the top center of the cake springs back. If the indentation remains, return the cakes to the oven for 2 minutes, or until the center springs back. Remove the cakes from the pans, and allow them to cool completely before frosting.

For the blueberry buttercream, make the batch of Swiss Meringue Buttercream, add the vanilla bean paste and blueberry preserves and mix until they're fully incorporated.

Place the first layer of cake on a flat surface and use an offset spatula with half of the frosting to frost the first and then the second layer of cake. Place the third layer on top, then smooth out any buttercream that squeezed out between the layers. Apply a thin crumb coat to the outside of the cake, and refrigerate the cake for at least 30 minutes.

Place the rest of the buttercream on top of the cake, and work it down the sides with an offset spatula. Use a cake scraper to smooth out the top and sides of the cake as needed.

This Blueberry Cardamom Cake is best served at room temperature. Store it in an airtight container in the fridge for up to a week.

YIELD: 8–10 SLICES

CARDAMOM CAKE
2¼ cups (270 g) all-purpose flour, spooned and leveled

2½ tsp (12 g) baking powder

½ tsp salt

¾ tsp cardamom

¾ tsp cinnamon

¼ cup (56 g) unsalted butter, room temperature

½ cup (120 ml) canola oil

½ cup (100 g) granulated sugar

1 cup packed (190 g) brown sugar

3 large eggs, room temperature

¾ cup (170 g) sour cream

1 tsp vanilla extract

¾ cup (180 ml) milk, room temperature

BLUEBERRY SWISS MERINGUE BUTTERCREAM
1 batch of Swiss Meringue Buttercream (page 13)

1 tbsp (13 g) vanilla bean paste or high-quality vanilla extract

½ cup (170 g) blueberry preserves (I use Bonne Maman Intense Blueberry Fruit Spread)

DARK CHOCOLATE
MARBLE CAKE

Marble cake is perfect for me because I'm one of those people who loves both vanilla and chocolate equally, and I can never decide between the two. That made it really hard to choose just one flavor for the buttercream used in this recipe. Although I could've done both, I went with a dark chocolate because, well, you just can't go wrong with a rich and silky dark chocolate buttercream.

For the cake, preheat the oven to 350°F (177°C). Grease three 6-inch (15-cm) cake pans with baking spray, and line them with parchment paper.

In a medium bowl, whisk together 2 cups (240 g) of the flour, the baking powder and salt.

In the bowl of a stand mixer fitted with the whisk attachment, beat the butter, oil and sugar on medium speed, until they're light and fluffy. This should take 2 to 3 minutes. Then add the eggs, one at a time, beating well after each addition for about 30 seconds. Make sure to scrape down the bottom and sides of the bowl as needed. Add the sour cream and vanilla, and mix just until they're combined.

With the mixer at low speed, add half of the dry ingredients to the mixture, followed by the milk and then the second half of the dry ingredients. Increase the mixer speed to medium, and beat the mixture, just until the flour is fully incorporated, making sure to scrape the flour from the sides of the bowl.

Divide the batter in half. To one half, add the remaining ¼ cup (30 g) of flour, mixing just until it's combined. To the other half, add the cocoa powder, mixing just until it's combined.

Alternating the vanilla and the chocolate batter, use a small ladle or ice cream scoop to put dabs of the batter in the pans. Fill the pans about one-half to two-thirds full. Then use a knife to swirl the chocolate and vanilla batter together to create a marbled effect.

Bake the cakes for about 35 minutes, until an indentation made with your finger in the top center of the cake springs back. If the indentation remains, return the cakes to the oven for 2 minutes, or until the center springs back. Remove the cakes from the pans, and allow them to cool completely before frosting.

(Continued)

YIELD: 8–10 SLICES

MARBLE CAKE
2¼ cups (270 g) all-purpose flour, spooned and leveled, divided

2½ tsp (12 g) baking powder

½ tsp salt

¼ cup (56 g) unsalted butter, room temperature

½ cup (120 ml) canola oil

1½ cups (300 g) granulated sugar

3 large eggs, room temperature

¾ cup (170 g) sour cream

1 tsp vanilla extract

¾ cup (180 ml) milk, room temperature

⅓ cup (26 g) Dutch-process cocoa powder, spooned and leveled

Make the batch of Thick Dark Chocolate Ganache, and set it aside to cool.

For the buttercream, melt the dark chocolate chips in a small bowl in the microwave for 20-second intervals, stirring after each interval, until it's completely smooth, 1 to 2 minutes. Allow it to cool while you make the batch of French Buttercream. When the buttercream is complete, add the cooled chocolate, vanilla bean paste and cocoa powder; mix until they're fully incorporated.

Place the first layer of cake on a flat surface and use an offset spatula with half of the frosting to frost the first and then the second layer of cake. Drizzle a generous layer of ganache on each layer of buttercream before stacking the layers. Place the third cake layer on top, then smooth out any buttercream that squeezed out between the layers. Apply a thin crumb coat to the outside of the cake, and refrigerate the cake for at least 30 minutes.

Place the rest of the buttercream on top of the cake and, with the offset spatula, work the buttercream down the sides. Place dabs of the Chocolate Ganache on top of the buttercream, and use the offset spatula to make swoops and swirls, blending the ganache only a little into the buttercream.

This Dark Chocolate Marble Cake is best served at room temperature. Store it in an airtight container in the fridge for up to a week.

CHOCOLATE GANACHE
1 batch of Thick Dark Chocolate Ganache (page 21)

DARK CHOCOLATE FRENCH BUTTERCREAM
½ cup (87 g) dark chocolate chips

1 batch of French Buttercream (page 15)

1 tbsp (13 g) vanilla bean paste or high-quality vanilla extract

½ cup (40 g) unsweetened cocoa powder, spooned and leveled

PEANUT BUTTER & JELLY CAKE

If you can't tell by now, I love nostalgic flavors, and I've been wanting to make a peanut butter and jelly cake for so long! I kept the cake layers vanilla so we could really bring out that peanut butter and jelly flavor through the frosting and filling. The frosting is a silky Peanut Butter Russian Buttercream and I snuck a little grown-up bourbon touch into the classic strawberry jam.

For the strawberry jam, in a medium saucepan, stir together the strawberries, sugar, water and salt. Bring the mixture to a boil over medium heat. Reduce the heat to low. Cook the strawberry jam for about 40 minutes, stirring occasionally. Once the jam begins to lose its liquid and deepen in color, remove it from the heat. If you pour it into a measuring cup, you should have about 1¼ cups (425 g) of strawberry jam. Stir in the bourbon and the vanilla bean paste until they're fully combined. Cover, allow the jam to cool to room temperature, then refrigerate it.

For the cake, preheat the oven to 350°F (177°C). Grease three 6-inch (15-cm) cake pans, and line them with parchment paper.

In a medium bowl, whisk together the flour, baking powder and salt.

In the bowl of a stand mixer fitted with the whisk attachment, beat the butter, oil, granulated and brown sugars on medium speed, until they're light and fluffy. This should take 2 to 3 minutes. Then add the eggs, one at a time, beating well after each addition for about 30 seconds. Make sure to scrape the bottom and sides of the bowl as needed. Add the sour cream and vanilla, and mix just until they're combined.

With the mixer at low speed, add half of the dry ingredients to the mixture, followed by the milk and then the second half of the dry ingredients. Increase the mixer speed to medium, and beat the mixture just until the flour is fully incorporated, making sure to scrape down the sides of the bowl as needed.

(Continued)

YIELD: 8–10 SLICES

BOURBON STRAWBERRY JAM

3 cups (425 g) strawberries, chopped

1 cup (200 g) granulated sugar

½ cup (120 ml) water

¼ tsp salt

1 tbsp (15 ml) bourbon

1 tsp vanilla bean paste or high-quality vanilla extract

VANILLA CAKE

2¼ cups (270 g) all-purpose flour

2½ tsp (12 g) baking powder

½ tsp salt

¼ cup (56 g) unsalted butter, room temperature

½ cup (120 ml) canola oil

½ cup (100 g) granulated sugar

1 cup (190 g) packed brown sugar

3 large eggs, room temperature

¾ cup (170 g) sour cream

1 tsp vanilla extract

¾ cup (180 ml) milk, room temperature

Distribute the batter evenly among the prepared pans, filling each pan only about one-half to three-quarters full. Bake the cakes for about 35 minutes, until an indentation made with your finger in the top center of the cake springs back. If the indentation remains, return the cakes back to the oven for 2 minutes, or until the center springs back. Remove the cakes from the pans, and allow them to cool completely before frosting.

For the Peanut Butter Buttercream, make the batch of Russian Buttercream. Add the vanilla bean paste and peanut butter, and mix until they're fully incorporated.

Place the first layer of cake on a flat surface and use an offset spatula to frost it with one-fourth of the buttercream. Pipe a border of frosting around the edge of the layer, then fill it in with about half of the strawberry jam. Repeat for the second layer. Place the third layer on top, then smooth out any buttercream that squeezed out between the layers. Apply a thin crumb coat to the outside of the cake, and refrigerate it for at least 30 minutes.

Place the rest of the buttercream on top of the cake, and use an offset spatula to work it down the sides. Use a cake scraper to smooth out the top and sides of the cake as needed.

This Peanut Butter & Jelly Cake is best served at room temperature or slightly chilled. Store it in an airtight container in the fridge for up to a week.

PEANUT BUTTER RUSSIAN BUTTERCREAM

1 batch of Russian Buttercream (page 18)

1 tsp vanilla bean paste or high-quality vanilla extract

½ cup (115 g) creamy peanut butter (I use Jif)

CARAMEL PEACHES 'N' CREAM CAKE

This cake is perfect during the transition from summer to fall. The peaches, light Ermine Buttercream (page 17) and whipped cream on top are light and summery. The warm and cozy brown sugar cake drizzled with the caramel sauce evokes fall. This one is a crowd-pleaser, for sure!

Begin by making the custard for the Ermine Buttercream at least a few hours before frosting the cake, so it has time to cool.

For the caramel sauce, place the sugar and water in a medium, light-colored saucepan with a lid over medium heat. Melt the sugar in the water, but DO NOT STIR IT. After about 10 minutes, the sugar will turn an amber color. Remove the mixture from the stove, and stir in the cream. The mixture will bubble violently, so be careful. Stir the mixture until it's completely combined, then whisk in the butter and pour the caramel into a heatproof bowl. Add the vanilla and salt, mixing until they're completely combined. Cover the caramel, and allow it to cool to room temperature.

For the cake, preheat the oven to 350°F (177°C). Grease two 8-inch (20-cm) cake pans with baking spray, and line them with parchment paper.

(Continued)

YIELD: 12—16 SLICES

VANILLA ERMINE BUTTERCREAM
1 batch of Ermine Buttercream (page 17)

1 tsp vanilla bean paste or high-quality vanilla extract

SALTED CARAMEL SAUCE
1 cup (200 g) granulated sugar

¼ cup (60 ml) water

½ cup (120 ml) heavy whipping cream, room temperature

¼ cup (56 g) unsalted butter, room temperature

½ tsp vanilla extract

½ tsp salt

CARAMEL PEACHES 'N' CREAM CAKE
(Continued)

In a medium bowl, whisk together the flour, baking powder, salt and cinnamon.

In the bowl of a stand mixer fitted with the whisk attachment, beat the butter, oil and brown sugar together, on medium speed, until they're light and fluffy. This should take 2 to 3 minutes. Then add the eggs, one at a time, beating well after each addition for about 30 seconds. Scrape down the bottom and sides of the bowl as needed. Add the sour cream and vanilla, and mix just until they're combined.

With the mixer at low speed, add half of the dry ingredients to the mixture, followed by the milk and then the second half of the dry ingredients. Increase the mixer speed to medium, then beat the mixture, just until the flour is fully incorporated, making sure to scrape the flour from the sides of the bowl.

Distribute the batter evenly among the pans, filling each pan only about one-half to two-thirds full. Bake the cakes for about 35 minutes, until an indentation made with your finger in the top center of the cake springs back. If the indentation remains, return the cakes to the oven for 2 minutes, or until the center springs back. Remove the cakes from the pans and allow them to cool completely.

Finish the Ermine Buttercream, then add the vanilla bean paste; mix until it's evenly distributed.

For the whipped cream, use an electric mixer, at full speed, to beat the cream with the powdered sugar until soft peaks form. Add the vanilla bean paste to the whipped cream and beat again, at full speed, just until stiff peaks form.

To frost, cut the cooled cakes in half horizontally to make four cake layers. Use an offset spatula to spread one-third of the buttercream onto the first layer of cake. Top the buttercream with a layer of sliced peaches, followed by a generous drizzle of caramel sauce. Repeat for the second and third layers of the cake. Place the fourth layer on top. Spread the whipped cream on the fourth layer of cake and then top with the extra fruit and another drizzle of caramel. Refrigerate the cake for at least 30 minutes before slicing it.

This Caramel Peaches 'n' Cream Cake is best served at room temperature or slightly chilled. Store it in an airtight container in the fridge for up to a week.

BROWN SUGAR CAKE
2¼ cups (270 g) all-purpose flour, spooned and leveled

2½ tsp (12 g) baking powder

½ tsp salt

2 tsp (4 g) cinnamon

¼ cup (56 g) unsalted butter, room temperature

½ cup (120 ml) canola oil

1½ cups (285 g) packed brown sugar

3 large eggs, room temperature

¾ cup (170 g) sour cream

1 tsp vanilla extract

¾ cup (180 ml) milk, room temperature

WHIPPED CREAM
1 cup (240 ml) heavy whipping cream, cold

2 tbsp (16 g) powdered sugar, spooned and leveled

½ tsp vanilla bean paste

TOPPING
3 large peaches (not superripe and juicy), thinly sliced

Handful of cherries, blackberries and/or pecans

LEMON VANILLA BEAN CAKE

Next to chocolate, I'm pretty sure lemon is the best flavor for desserts. The sweet and tart combination is just heavenly. In this recipe, I paired a tangy lemon curd with a classic vanilla cake and vanilla American Meringue Buttercream (page 12). Vanilla is a pretty subtle flavor, making it the perfect balance for a sweet and sour lemon curd.

For the lemon curd, stir together the lemon zest and juice, egg, egg yolk, sugar, butter and salt in a small saucepan. Over medium-low heat, whisk the mixture continuously for 5 to 10 minutes, until it becomes thick enough to coat the back of a spoon. Pour the lemon curd into a heatproof bowl, cover the surface with plastic wrap to prevent it from forming a skin and allow it to cool completely to room temperature, about 2 hours, then refrigerate it.

For the cake, preheat the oven to 350°F (177°C). Grease three 6-inch (15-cm) cake pans with baking spray, and line them with parchment paper.

In a medium bowl, whisk together the flour, baking powder and salt.

In the bowl of a stand mixer fitted with the whisk attachment, beat the butter, oil and sugar together, on medium speed, until they're light and fluffy. This should take 2 to 3 minutes. Then add the eggs, one at a time, beating well after each addition for about 30 seconds. Scrape down the bottom and sides of the bowl as needed. Add the sour cream and vanilla, and mix just until they're combined.

With the mixer at low speed, add half of the dry ingredients to the mixture, followed by the milk and then the second half of the dry ingredients. Beat the mixture on medium speed, just until the flour is fully incorporated, scraping down the flour from the sides of the bowl.

Distribute the batter evenly among the prepared pans, filling each pan only about one-half to two-thirds full. Bake the cakes for about 35 minutes, until an indentation made with your finger in the top center of the cake springs back. If the indentation remains, return the cakes to the oven for 2 minutes, or until the center springs back. Remove the cakes from the pans. Allow them to cool completely before frosting.

(Continued)

YIELD: 8—10 SLICES

LEMON CURD
Zest of 1 large lemon

¼ cup (60 ml) freshly squeezed lemon juice

1 large egg

1 large egg yolk

¼ cup (50 g) granulated sugar

3 tbsp (42 g) unsalted butter, softened

⅛ tsp salt

VANILLA CAKE
2¼ cups (270 g) all-purpose flour, spooned and leveled

2½ tsp (12 g) baking powder

½ tsp salt

¼ cup (56 g) unsalted butter, room temperature

½ cup (120 ml) canola oil

1½ cups (300 g) granulated sugar

3 large eggs, room temperature

¾ cup (170 g) sour cream

2 tsp (10 ml) vanilla extract

¾ cup (180 ml) milk, room temperature

LEMON VANILLA BEAN CAKE *(Continued)*

Make the American Meringue Buttercream, then stir in the vanilla bean paste until it's evenly distributed.

Place the first layer of cake on a flat surface and use an offset spatula to spread a layer of buttercream on top. Use a piping bag to pipe a border of buttercream around the edges and then fill the center with lemon curd. Repeat for the second layer of the cake. Place the third layer on top, then gently smooth out any buttercream that squeezed out between the layers. Refrigerate the cake for 1 hour, and then apply a thin crumb coat to the outside of the cake. Refrigerate the cake for at least 30 minutes.

Place the rest of the buttercream on top of the cake and, with the offset spatula, work it down the sides. With a cake scraper, smooth out the top and sides of the cake as needed, and then use a cake decorating comb to create stripes in the buttercream. Top with the lemon zest and slices.

This Lemon Vanilla Bean Cake is best served at room temperature or slightly chilled. Store it in an airtight container in the fridge for up to a week.

VANILLA AMERICAN MERINGUE BUTTERCREAM
1 batch of American Meringue Buttercream (page 12)

1 tbsp (13 g) vanilla bean paste

TOPPING
Zest of ½ of small lemon

2 slices of lemon

SWEET
SHEETS

Ohhhh, sheet cakes: They really are so sweet. They are supereasy to make and still on par with the taste of a layer cake. It really is the best of both worlds. Not to mention—as with layer cakes—you'll never run out of flavor combinations.

Sheet cakes are generally made in sheet pans that are 18 x 24 inches (45 x 60 cm), which is almost four times the size of the pan I used for most of these recipes. I find that most home bakers prefer to bake in smaller quantities, so most of these recipes will make a 9 x 13–inch (33 x 23–cm) cake. You can absolutely multiply the recipe or bake multiple cakes, if needed.

I also included a couple of layered sheet cakes. They're significantly shorter than my layer cakes, but they're meant to be sliced and served as a sheet cake. Just think of it as an impressive but easy layer cake, and remember that no one is complaining about that extra layer of deliciousness!

Sheet cakes make for an easy way to experiment with different frostings, such as interchanging buttercreams and flavors. You don't have to worry about a frosting being too soft to hold up a layer cake or stand too tall on top of a cupcake. It's also great to practice your piping skills on sheet cakes, because if you mess up you can easily just spread it out and create swirls or try again.

BUTTERSCOTCH CHOCOLATE CHIP CAKE

I really wanted to make a chocolate chip cake, but I thought plain chocolate chip vanilla cake was a bit boring. So, to take this cake from boring to exceptional, I not only added butterscotch chips to the batter, I also made a homemade butterscotch sauce to infuse into the silky Swiss Meringue Buttercream (page 13).

For the Butterscotch Sauce, in a small saucepan over medium-low heat, melt the butter and sugar, whisking until it's smooth. Bring the mixture to a boil—it should take only 1 to 2 minutes—whisking intermittently. Pour in the cream, bring the mixture back to a boil for 1 minute and then remove it from the heat. Pour the sauce into a heatproof bowl. Add the vanilla and salt, mixing just until they're incorporated. Cover the sauce and allow it to cool to room temperature.

For the cake, preheat the oven to 350°F (177°C). Grease a 9 x 13 x 2–inch (33 x 23 x 5–cm) cake pan with baking spray, and line it with parchment paper.

In a medium bowl, whisk together the flour, baking powder and salt. Remove and reserve 1 tablespoon (7 g) of the mixture, then set aside the bowl of dry ingredients.

In the bowl of a stand mixer fitted with the whisk attachment, beat the butter, oil and granulated and brown sugars together, on medium speed, until they're light and fluffy. This should take 2 to 3 minutes. Then add the eggs, one at a time, beating well after each addition for about 30 seconds. Make sure to scrape down the bottom and sides of the bowl as needed. Add the sour cream and vanilla, and mix just until they're combined.

With the mixer at low speed, add half of the dry ingredients to the mixture, followed by the milk and then the second half of the dry ingredients. Beat the mixture on medium speed, just until the flour is fully incorporated, making sure to scrape down the flour from the sides of the bowl. In a small bowl, toss the butterscotch chips and chocolate chips with the reserved flour until they're coated, then fold them into the batter until they're evenly distributed.

(Continued)

YIELD: 24 PIECES

BUTTERSCOTCH SAUCE

½ cup (113 g) unsalted butter, softened

1 cup (190 g) packed brown sugar

¼ cup (60 ml) heavy whipping cream, room temperature

½ tsp vanilla extract

¼ tsp salt

CHOCOLATE CHIP BUTTERSCOTCH CAKE

2¼ cups (270 g) all-purpose flour, spooned and leveled

2½ tsp (12 g) baking powder

½ tsp salt

¼ cup (56 g) unsalted butter, room temperature

½ cup (120 ml) canola oil

¾ cup (150 g) granulated sugar

¾ cup (142 g) packed light brown sugar

3 large eggs, room temperature

¾ cup (170 g) sour cream

1 tbsp (15 ml) vanilla extract

¾ cup (180 ml) milk, room temperature

¾ cup (130 g) butterscotch chips

¾ cup (130 g) semisweet chocolate chips

Pour the batter into the prepared pan, and bake the cake for about 35 minutes, until an indentation made with your finger in the top center of the cake springs back. If the indentation remains, return the cake to the oven for 2 minutes, or until the center springs back. Remove the cake from the oven and allow it to cool in the pan for 30 minutes. Then, remove it from the pan, and place it on a flat surface to finish cooling.

For the butterscotch buttercream, make the batch of Swiss Meringue Buttercream. Add ½ cup (120 ml) of the Butterscotch Sauce and the vanilla bean paste, and mix just until they're fully incorporated.

Spread all of the frosting on top of the cake, and drizzle it with extra butterscotch sauce. If you have leftover sauce, store it, covered, in the fridge for up to a month. Top the cake with the chocolate chips, and slice into even squares.

This Butterscotch Chocolate Chip Cake is best served at room temperature. Store it in an airtight container in the fridge for up to a week.

BUTTERSCOTCH
SWISS MERINGUE
BUTTERCREAM
1 batch of Swiss Meringue Buttercream (page 13)

1 tsp vanilla bean paste or high-quality vanilla extract

TOPPING
¼ cup (44 g) mini chocolate chips or chocolate shavings

LITTLE MOCHA CAKE

This is another recipe inspired by cakes I grew up eating! My mom makes a two-layer, milk and dark chocolate sponge cake, filled with chocolate Diplomat Cream (page 23) and dunked in Dark Chocolate Ganache (page 21). It's extra chocolaty, but instead of being rich and dark, it's light and creamy. She also makes a coffee cake that's pretty similar, but uses white cake with coffee syrup and Espresso Diplomat Cream. I combined the two to make the ultimate mocha sponge cake!

Begin by making the custard for the batches of Diplomat Cream at least a few hours before frosting the cake, so it has time to cool.

For the Coffee Soak, stir the sugar into the coffee until it's dissolved. Let the syrup cool completely, then refrigerate it until it's ready to be used.

For the cake, preheat the oven to 350°F (177°C), and arrange racks at the top and middle of the oven. Grease three 10-inch (25-cm) square baking pans with baking spray.

In a small bowl, whisk together the flour, cocoa powder, baking powder and salt.

Using the whisk attachment on your stand mixer, beat the egg whites and sugar on high speed for 1 to 2 minutes, until they look really fluffy. Reduce the speed to medium, add the egg yolks and vanilla and mix until they're fully combined. Stop the mixer and sift half of the dry ingredients over the batter. Beat the mixture at low speed, just until the flour mixture is mostly incorporated. Repeat with the remaining flour mixture, making sure to scrape down the sides of the bowl. Don't overmix; you want the batter to be light and very fluffy.

Divide the batter among the prepared baking pans. Bake the cakes, on the top and middle racks of the oven, for 12 to 14 minutes, or until an indentation made with your finger in the top center of the cakes springs back. Remove the cakes from the oven, flip them onto cooling racks and allow them to cool completely.

(Continued)

(Continued)

YIELD: 12 PIECES

ESPRESSO DIPLOMAT CREAM
2 batches of Diplomat Cream (page 23)

2 tbsp (12 g) espresso powder dissolved in 1 tbsp (15 ml) hot water, then cooled

1 tsp vanilla bean paste or high-quality vanilla extract

COFFEE SOAK
¼ cup (50 g) granulated sugar

1½ cups (360 ml) brewed coffee, hot

CHOCOLATE SPONGE
¾ cup (90 g) all-purpose flour, spooned and leveled

½ cup (40 g) cocoa powder, spooned and leveled

1 tsp baking powder

¼ tsp salt

8 large eggs, separated and room temperature, divided

¾ cup (150 g) granulated sugar

1 tsp vanilla extract

For the Espresso Diplomat Cream, finish making the Diplomat Cream, then add the espresso mixture and the vanilla bean paste. Mix just until the ingredients are fully incorporated.

Place one cake on a flat surface and use a spoon to drizzle over one-third of the Coffee Soak to soak the cake. Spread one-third of the Espresso Diplomat Cream on top, then repeat with the remaining two layers. Refrigerate the cake for at least 30 minutes.

Make the half batch of Thin Dark Chocolate Ganache while the cake chills. Let the ganache cool just until it's not warm, but is still thin enough to drizzle, 5 to 10 minutes.

Generously drizzle the top of the cake with the ganache. Refrigerate the cake for at least 4 hours. Slice the cake into even squares.

This Little Mocha Cake is best served chilled. Store it in an airtight container in the fridge for up to a week.

CHOCOLATE GANACHE
½ batch of Thin Dark Chocolate Ganache (page 21)

BROWN BUTTER
BIRTHDAY CAKE

Is there anything prettier than funfetti cake? I didn't think so. Is there anything better than brown butter? Also didn't think so. Sprinkles make everything prettier, and brown butter gives any dish, sweet or savory, a more interesting and nuttier flavor. It's the perfect addition when you want to elevate a classic or boring dish. In this recipe, I also wanted to show you that you can make European buttercreams using brown butter.

For the Brown Butter, cook the butter in a small saucepan over medium heat, stirring the butter frequently, until it begins to foam, about 5 minutes. Stir the butter continuously at this point. Soon, you will see the milk solids browning and settling toward the bottom of the pan. The smell will also begin to change to a nutty aroma. At about 10 minutes, when the butter turns an amber color with brown speckles, quickly remove it from the heat and pour it into a large heatproof bowl. Cool the butter completely at room temperature, then refrigerate it for 1 hour before using it.

For the cake, preheat the oven to 350°F (177°C). Grease a 9 x 13 x 2–inch (33 x 23 x 5–cm) cake pan with baking spray, then line it with parchment paper.

In a medium bowl, whisk together the flour, baking powder and salt.

In the bowl of a stand mixer fitted with the whisk attachment, beat ¼ cup (56 g) of the chilled brown butter with the oil and granulated sugar, on medium speed, until they're light and fluffy. This should take 2 to 3 minutes. Then add the eggs, one at a time, beating well after each addition for about 30 seconds. Make sure to scrape down the bottom and sides of the bowl as needed. Add the sour cream and vanilla, and mix just until they're combined.

With the mixer at low speed, add half of the dry ingredients to the butter mixture, followed by the milk and then the second half of the dry ingredients, mixing just until the flour is barely combined. Add the sprinkles, and mix them on low speed until they're evenly distributed in the batter.

(Continued)

YIELD: 24 PIECES

BROWN BUTTER
1 cup (227 g) unsalted butter

BROWN BUTTER SPRINKLE CAKE
2¼ cups (270 g) all-purpose flour, spooned and leveled

2½ tsp (12 g) baking powder

½ tsp salt

½ cup (120 ml) canola oil

1½ cups (300 g) granulated sugar

3 large eggs, room temperature

¾ cup (170 g) sour cream

1 tbsp (15 ml) vanilla extract

¾ cup (180 ml) milk, room temperature

⅓ cup (50 g) rainbow sequin sprinkles

Pour the batter into the prepared pan, and bake the cake for about 35 minutes, until an indentation made with your finger in the top center of the cake springs back. If the indentation remains, return the cake to the oven for 2 minutes, or until the center springs back. Remove the cake from the oven, and allow it to cool in the pan for 30 minutes. Then, remove it from the pan, and place it on a flat surface to finish cooling.

For the brown butter buttercream, if the brown butter is solid, remove it from the refrigerator until it warms to the consistency of room temperature butter. Make the Italian Meringue Buttercream, using ½ cup (113 g) of the room temperature brown butter along with half of the butter (½ cup [113 g]) in the base recipe. Add the vanilla bean paste and extract, and mix until they're incorporated.

Spread the buttercream on top of the cooled cake, then top the frosting with the sprinkles. Cut the cake into even squares.

This Brown Butter Birthday Cake is best served at room temperature. Store it in an airtight container in the fridge for up to a week.

TIP:
If you have leftover Brown Butter, refrigerate it and try it with savory foods, such as vegetables.

BROWN BUTTER
ITALIAN
MERINGUE
BUTTERCREAM
1 batch of Italian Meringue Buttercream (page 14), substitute Brown Butter for half of the butter

1 tsp vanilla bean paste or high-quality vanilla extract

½ tsp artificial clear vanilla extract

2 tbsp (20 g) rainbow sequin sprinkles

DARK CHOCOLATE GUINNESS CAKE

If you've never had a chocolate stout cake, then you're in for a pleasant surprise! Stout carries notes of coffee and chocolate, so it pairs well with this dark chocolate cake. I chose a French Buttercream (page 15) for this cake, because its rich and luscious texture pairs well with the light and spongy texture of the chocolate cake.

To make the chocolate cake, preheat the oven to 350°F (177°C). Grease a 9 x 13 x 2-inch (33 x 23 x 5-cm) cake pan with baking spray, and line it with parchment paper.

In a medium bowl, whisk together the flour, granulated and brown sugars, cocoa powder, baking soda, baking powder and salt.

In a large bowl, whisk together the eggs, oil, buttermilk, Guinness and vanilla until they're well combined. Sift the dry ingredients over the wet mixture, then fold them together just until the last streak of flour is combined.

Pour the batter into the prepared pan. Bake the cake for 35 to 40 minutes, until an indentation made with your finger in the top center of the cake springs back. If the indentation remains, return the cake to the oven for 2 minutes, or until the center springs back. Remove the cake from the oven, and allow it to cool in the pan for 30 minutes. Then, remove it from the pan, and place it on a flat surface to finish cooling.

To make the Chocolate Stout Ganache, combine the chocolate chips, Guinness and butter in a heatproof bowl, and melt them together over a double boiler, stirring, until the mixture is smooth, about 5 minutes. Remove the bowl from the heat, cover it with a lid or plastic wrap and set it aside to cool.

(Continued)

GUINNESS CAKE
1½ cups (180 g) all-purpose flour, spooned and leveled

1 cup (200 g) granulated sugar

1 cup (190 g) packed brown sugar

½ cup (40 g) unsweetened cocoa powder, spooned and leveled

1 tsp baking soda

1 tsp baking powder

½ tsp salt

2 large eggs, room temperature

½ cup (120 ml) canola oil

¾ cup (180 ml) buttermilk, room temperature

1¼ cups (300 ml) Guinness draught stout, room temperature

1 tsp vanilla extract

CHOCOLATE STOUT GANACHE
½ cup (87 g) dark chocolate chips

¼ cup (60 ml) Guinness draught stout, room temperature

2 tbsp (28 g) unsalted butter, softened

DARK CHOCOLATE GUINNESS
CAKE *(Continued)*

For the chocolate buttercream, make the batch of French Buttercream, then sift in the cocoa powder and add the vanilla bean paste. Mix just until they're fully combined.

Once the cake has fully cooled, use a chopstick or something of similar size to poke small holes into the cake, 1 to 2 inches (2.5 to 5 cm) apart and going only halfway down through the cake. Spread about two-thirds of the Chocolate Stout Ganache over the cake, letting it drip into the holes. Spread the chocolate buttercream on top of the cake, then drizzle the remaining one-third of the ganache on top of the buttercream. Refrigerate the cake for 30 minutes, then cut it into even squares.

This Dark Chocolate Guinness Cake is best served at room temperature. Store it in an airtight container in the fridge for up to a week.

CHOCOLATE FRENCH BUTTERCREAM
1 batch of French Buttercream (page 15)

¼ cup (20 g) cocoa powder, spooned and leveled

1 tsp vanilla bean paste or high-quality vanilla extract

BANANA SNICKERDOODLE CAKE

This banana sheet cake is so incredibly moist. Its cinnamon sugar swirl, which caramelizes on the edge of the pan, takes it to the next level. The only thing that could make this cake better is a gorgeous cloud of frosting on top. I provided just that with a Cinnamon Ermine Buttercream. It's superlight and fluffy, making it the perfect balance for banana cake.

Begin by making the custard for the Ermine Buttercream at least a few hours before frosting the cake, so it has time to cool.

For the cake, preheat the oven to 350°F (177°C). Grease a 9 x 13 x 2–inch (33 x 23 x 5–cm) cake pan with baking spray, and line it with parchment paper.

In a medium bowl, whisk together the flour, baking soda, baking powder, salt and cinnamon.

In a large bowl, whisk together the granulated and brown sugars and the eggs, until the mixture is smooth. Add the Greek yogurt, oil and vanilla, whisking them until they're fully incorporated. Add the bananas to the mixture, and mix until they're fully combined. Add the dry ingredients, and mix until the flour is just barely incorporated.

For the Cinnamon Sugar Swirl, combine the brown sugar and cinnamon in a medium bowl.

Pour half of the banana cake batter into the prepared pan, top with an even layer of the cinnamon swirl, then pour the other half of the batter on top. Bake the cake for about 40 minutes, until an indentation made with your finger in the top center of the cake springs back. If the indentation remains, return the cake to the oven for 2 minutes, or until the center springs back. Remove the cake from the oven, and allow it to cool in the pan for 30 minutes. Remove the cake from the pan, and place it on a flat surface to finish cooling.

Finish the Ermine Buttercream, then add the vanilla bean paste and cinnamon. Mix just until they're fully incorporated.

When the cake has cooled, frost the cake with the buttercream. Refrigerate the cake for 30 minutes, then cut it into 24 pieces.

This Banana Snickerdoodle Cake is best served at room temperature or slightly chilled. Cover any cut pieces with plastic wrap, and store them in the refrigerator.

YIELD: 24 PIECES

CINNAMON ERMINE BUTTERCREAM
1 batch of Ermine Buttercream (page 17)

1 tsp vanilla bean paste or high-quality vanilla extract

1 tsp cinnamon

BANANA CAKE
2½ cups (300 g) all-purpose flour, spooned and leveled

½ tsp baking soda

2 tsp (7 g) baking powder

½ tsp salt

1 tsp cinnamon

1 cup (200 g) granulated sugar

½ cup (95 g) packed brown sugar

2 large eggs, room temperature

½ cup (113 g) Greek yogurt

½ cup (120 ml) canola oil

1 tsp vanilla extract

3 large ripe bananas, mashed

CINNAMON SUGAR SWIRL
½ cup (95 g) packed brown sugar

1 tsp cinnamon

VANILLA CUSTARD CAKE

Bavarian Cream (page 22) could be a type of frosting or just a dessert on its own, and you really can't go wrong using it between two layers of buttery, flaky pastry. It's a superlight and fluffy cream, but still sets well in the fridge, so you're able to pile this whipped custard topping nice and high!

YIELD: 24 PIECES

1 batch of Bavarian Cream (page 22)

1 sheet of puff pastry (I use Pepperidge Farm), thawed, room temperature

1 tbsp (13 g) vanilla bean paste or high-quality vanilla extract

Powdered sugar

Begin by making the custard for the Bavarian Cream and set aside for a few hours to cool completely.

For the pastry, preheat the oven to 425°F (218°C). On a sheet of parchment paper, use a rolling pin to gently smooth out the creases in the puff pastry dough, then stretch it out an extra inch or two (2.5 or 5 cm).

Transfer the pastry on the parchment paper to an 18 x 13–inch (46 x 33–cm) baking sheet. Bake the pastry for 10 minutes. Reduce the oven temperature to 375°F (190°C), and bake the pastry for 10 to 15 minutes, until the pastry is beginning to look slightly darker than golden brown. Remove the pastry from the oven, and allow it to cool completely to room temperature.

Finish making the Bavarian Cream, then add the vanilla bean paste, mixing just until it's evenly distributed.

Once the puff pastry is cool, use a large serrated knife to slice it into two parts, a top and a bottom, leaving about two-thirds of the puff pastry for the bottom and one-third for the top. Use your hands to crumble the top section of the puff pastry into a bowl; set it aside. Cover the whole bottom pastry with the Bavarian cream, then sprinkle the crumbled pastry on top of the cream.

Refrigerate the cake for at least 3 to 4 hours, until the cream is firm. Dust the top of the cake with the powdered sugar, and cut it into even squares.

This Vanilla Custard Cake is best served slightly chilled. Store it in an airtight container in the fridge for up to a week.

SALTED CARAMEL
GINGERBREAD CAKE

You didn't think I was going to write this book and not have some sort of holiday flavors in it, did you?! This gingerbread cake, frosted with a creamy caramel German Buttercream (page 16), is so good we were eating it in the middle of summer. And, if you've never paired gingerbread with caramel, you're missing out on an essential part of the holiday season . . . or summertime?

Begin by making the custard for the German Buttercream at least a few hours before frosting the cake, so it has time to cool.

To make the caramel sauce, place the sugar and water in a medium, light-colored saucepan with a lid over medium heat. Allow the sugar to melt in the water, but DO NOT STIR IT. After about 10 minutes, when the sugar begins to turn an amber color, remove it from the stove, and slowly stir in the cream. The mixture will bubble violently, so be careful. Stir the mixture until it's completely combined, then whisk in the butter and pour the caramel into a heatproof bowl. Add the salt and vanilla, mixing until they're completely combined. Cover the caramel, and allow it to cool to room temperature.

For the cake, preheat the oven to 350°F (177°C). Grease a 9 x 13 x 2–inch (33 x 23 x 5–cm) cake pan with baking spray, and line it with parchment paper.

(Continued)

YIELD: 24 PIECES

SALTED CARAMEL GERMAN BUTTERCREAM
1 batch of German Buttercream (page 16)

1 tsp vanilla bean paste or high-quality vanilla extract

Pinch of cinnamon

SALTED CARAMEL SAUCE
½ cup (100 g) granulated sugar

2 tbsp (30 ml) water

¼ cup (60 ml) heavy whipping cream, room temperature

2 tbsp (28 g) unsalted butter, softened

½ tsp salt

½ tsp vanilla extract

SALTED CARAMEL GINGERBREAD
CAKE *(Continued)*

In a medium bowl, whisk together the flour, baking powder, salt, cinnamon, ginger, nutmeg, cloves and allspice.

In the bowl of a stand mixer fitted with the whisk attachment, beat the butter, oil, brown sugar and molasses on medium speed, until they're light and fluffy. This should take 2 to 3 minutes. Then add the eggs, one at a time, beating well after each addition for about 30 seconds. Make sure to scrape down the bottom and sides of the bowl as needed. Add the sour cream and vanilla, and mix just until they're combined.

With the mixer at low speed, add half of the dry ingredients to the egg mixture, followed by the milk and then the second half of the dry ingredients. Increase the mixer speed to medium, then beat the mixture, just until the flour is fully incorporated, making sure to scrape the flour from the sides of the bowl.

Pour the batter into the prepared pan, and bake the cake for about 40 minutes, until an indentation made with your finger in the top center of the cake springs back. If the indentation remains, return the cake to the oven for 2 minutes, or until the center springs back. Remove the cake from the oven, and allow it to cool in the pan for 30 minutes. Then remove the cake from the pan, and place it on a flat surface to finish cooling.

For the buttercream, finish making the German Buttercream, then add the vanilla bean paste and ½ cup (148 g) of the cooled caramel sauce, mixing just until they're fully combined.

Scoop the buttercream into a piping bag fitted with a piping tip. Pipe random designs of buttercream onto the top of the cake, changing the tip as desired to create different textures. Dust the buttercream with the cinnamon, then drizzle the remaining caramel sauce on the cake. Refrigerate the cake for 30 minutes and cut into even squares.

This Salted Caramel Gingerbread Cake is best served at room temperature. Store it in an airtight container in the fridge for up to a week.

GINGERBREAD CAKE

2¼ cups (270 g) all-purpose flour, spooned and leveled

2½ tsp (12 g) baking powder

½ tsp salt

1½ tsp (3 g) cinnamon

1½ tsp (3 g) ginger

½ tsp nutmeg

½ tsp cloves

½ tsp allspice

¼ cup (56 g) unsalted butter, room temperature

½ cup (120 ml) canola oil

1½ cups (285 g) packed dark brown sugar

1 tbsp (21 g) molasses

3 large eggs, room temperature

¾ cup (170 g) sour cream

1 tbsp (15 ml) vanilla extract

¾ cup (180 ml) milk, room temperature

LEMON FRUIT CAKE

This cake screams summer! It's adapted from another one of my mom's most popular recipes: a light and fluffy sponge cake drenched in simple syrup, frosted with a Lemon Bavarian Cream and topped with fruit! There's a secret layer of pineapple in the middle that no one ever knows is there, but it makes all the difference in the end product. The best part about this cake is the play on sweet and sour from the tangy lemon cream and the fruits.

Begin by making the custard for the Bavarian Cream at least a few hours before frosting the cake, so it has time to cool.

For the cake, arrange a rack at the top and center of the oven, and preheat it to 350°F (177°C). Grease two 10-inch (25-cm) square baking pans with baking spray.

In a small bowl, whisk together the flour, baking soda and salt.

Use the stand mixer with a whisk attachment to beat the egg whites on high speed for 30 to 60 seconds, until they begin to look frothy. Add the sugar and continue beating the mixture on high speed for 1 to 2 minutes, until it's really fluffy. Reduce the speed to medium, and add the egg yolks and vanilla, mixing until they're fully combined.

Stop the mixer, and sift half of the dry ingredients over the batter. Beat the mixture at low speed, just until the flour mixture is mostly incorporated. Repeat with the second half, making sure to scrape down the sides of the bowl. Don't overmix; you want the batter to be light and very fluffy.

Fill the prepared baking pans. Bake the cakes on the top and middle racks of the oven for about 15 minutes, or until an indentation made with your finger in the top center of the cakes springs back. If the indentation remains, return the cake to the oven for 2 minutes, or until the center springs back. Remove the cakes from the oven, flip them onto a flat surface and and allow them to cool completely.

For the lemon cream, finish the Bavarian Cream, then add the lemon extract and lemon juice. Mix just until they're combined.

(Continued)

LEMON BAVARIAN CREAM
1 batch of Bavarian Cream (page 22)

1 tsp lemon extract

2 tsp (10 ml) lemon juice

SPONGE
1 cup (120 g) all-purpose flour, spooned and leveled

½ tsp baking soda

⅛ tsp salt

8 large eggs, separated and room temperature, divided

¾ cup (150 g) granulated sugar

½ tsp vanilla extract

For the filling, combine the reserved pineapple juice with the water. Place one sheet of cake on a flat surface, and spoon one-half of the juice mixture on it to soak the layer. Spread one-half of the Lemon Bavarian Cream on top, then place the pineapple on top of the cream, packing it full. Generously top the pineapple with the berries, then dab the top of the berries with a tiny bit of buttercream so the next layer will stick. Place the second layer of cake on top, and soak it with the remaining juice mixture. Frost the top of the cake with the remaining one-half of the Lemon Bavarian Cream.

Refrigerate the cake for at least 3 to 4 four hours, or overnight.

Cut the cake into even squares. Before serving the cake, beat the cream with the powdered sugar and vanilla bean paste until stiff peaks form. Use a spoon or a piping bag to place a dollop of the whipped cream on top of each slice of cake. Top with the fresh berries.

This Lemon Fruit Cake is best served chilled. Store it in an airtight container in the fridge for three to four days.

FILLING

1 (8-oz [227-g]) can crushed pineapple in pineapple juice, drained and with juice reserved

¾ cup (180 ml) water

1½ cups (180 g) mixed berries; dice only the strawberries

TOPPING

½ cup (120 ml) heavy whipping cream

1 tbsp (8 g) powdered sugar

½ tsp vanilla bean paste or high-quality vanilla extract

½ cup (60 g) whole mixed berries

PEANUT BUTTER CHOCOLATE CAKE

OK friends, I've said it before: not many things in life are better than chocolate and peanut butter. If you're not a believer, then you most certainly will be after you've tried this cake. This chocolate cake straight up melts in your mouth, and the Peanut Butter Swiss Meringue Buttercream, made with brown sugar, has got to be the creamiest, silkiest buttercream of all time. It's so incredibly fluffy, it's like eating a peanut butter cloud. This is definitely one of those cakes that you just won't be able to resist.

To make the chocolate cake, preheat the oven to 350°F (177°C). Grease a 9 x 13 x 2–inch (33 x 23 x 5–cm) cake pan with baking spray, and line it with parchment paper.

In a medium bowl, whisk together the flour, granulated and brown sugars, cocoa powder, baking soda, baking powder and salt.

In a large bowl, whisk together the eggs, oil, buttermilk, coffee and vanilla until they're well combined. Sift the dry ingredients over the egg mixture, and fold them together just until the last streak of flour is combined.

Pour the batter into the prepared pan, and bake the cake for 35 to 40 minutes, until an indentation made with your finger in the top center of the cake springs back. If the indentation remains, return the cake to the oven for 2 minutes, or until the center springs back. Remove the cake from the oven, and allow it to cool in the pan for 30 minutes. Remove the cake from the pan, and place it on a flat surface to finish cooling.

For the peanut butter buttercream, use brown sugar instead of granulated sugar to make the Swiss Meringue Buttercream; add the extra butter along with that from the base recipe. Add the peanut butter and vanilla bean paste to the buttercream, and mix just until they're fully combined.

Reserve ¼ cup (46 g) of the buttercream. Spread the remaining buttercream on top of the cake. Sift the cocoa powder over the reserved buttercream, and mix until it's fully combined. Use an offset spatula to place dabs of the chocolate cream on top of the cake, and swoop them to create decorative swirls.

Refrigerate the cake for 30 minutes, then cut it into even squares.

This Peanut Butter Chocolate Cake is best served at room temperature. Store it in an airtight container in the fridge for up to a week.

CHOCOLATE CAKE
1½ cups (180 g) all-purpose flour, spooned and leveled

1 cup (200 g) granulated sugar

1 cup (190 g) packed brown sugar

½ cup (40 g) Dutch-process cocoa powder, spooned and leveled

1 tsp baking soda

1 tsp baking powder

½ tsp salt

2 large eggs, room temperature

½ cup (120 ml) canola oil

1 cup (240 ml) buttermilk, room temperature

1 cup (240 ml) brewed coffee, room temperature

1 tsp vanilla extract

PEANUT BUTTER SWISS MERINGUE BUTTERCREAM
1 batch of Swiss Meringue Buttercream (page 13), made with light brown sugar instead of granulated sugar

2 tbsp (28 g) unsalted butter, room temperature, added with the butter in the base recipe

½ cup (115 g) creamy peanut butter (I use Jif)

1 tsp vanilla bean paste or high-quality vanilla extract

2 tbsp (10 g) cocoa powder, spooned and leveled

CUTIE
CUPCAKES

"Mini-cupcakes? As in the mini version of regular cupcakes, which is already a mini version of cake? Honestly, where does it end with you people?" If you can name that line and we're not already friends, can we be?

This chapter got its name because cupcakes are basically the cute little version of cakes . . . kind of like babies, the cute little version of you. As cute as these mini cakes are, they can also be so finicky! I've seen many people use any ol' cake recipe and bake it as cupcakes. But that's never worked for me, so I went on a wild adventure developing the ultimate base cupcake recipe.

Cupcakes need to have the perfect ratio of wet to dry to temperature to leavening, etc., in order to rise perfectly. Everyone's perfect cupcake is different, and I tested about twenty versions before I settled on my favorite basic white cupcake. I had multiple goals for my cupcake recipe. My cupcakes had to dome perfectly; be moist, even the next day; be easily adaptable to different flavors and be white, not yellow, with no brown edges. Cupcakes look nicer when they're white, and white batter is easier to color, if desired. I suggest a gel food coloring for that.

You can find the recipe for my basic white cupcake with the Chocolate Vanilla Hi-Hat Cupcakes (page 90) or the Almond Raspberry Cupcakes (page 93), where I just swap out almond extract for the vanilla.

And, can we talk about filled cupcakes for a second? There's nothing better than a surprise bite of Nutella (page 97) or cookie butter (page 98).

Several of my cupcake recipes yield a baker's dozen—a lucky thirteen. If your muffin tin makes twelve and you don't want to use a second tin, just discard the batter for the extra cupcake. Don't squeeze it into 12 tins, as your cupcakes won't bake properly.

OREO® LATTE CUPCAKES

You already know I'm all about flavor combinations. I rarely make just "chocolate cake." For me, it's something like "chocolate peanut butter cake" or "Guinness chocolate cake." The combination in this recipe has been one that I've loved for over 10 years. People think Oreos and milk are heavenly together, but I'm here to show you that Oreos have found a new best friend, and her name is coffee.

Begin by making the custard for the German Buttercream with the espresso powder, sugar and cornstarch mixture at least a few hours before frosting the cupcakes, so the custard has time to cool.

For the cupcakes, preheat the oven to 350°F (177°C), and line 13 muffin tins with paper liners.

Place the flour, sugar, baking soda, baking powder and salt in a large bowl, and whisk them together until the mixture is well combined. Add the butter and oil and use an electric mixer, on medium speed, to combine the mixture. Add the egg whites, and continue to beat the mixture until the egg whites are fully incorporated. Add the vanilla, milk and sour cream, beating the mixture on medium speed until the batter is fully combined. Make sure to scrape down the sides of the bowl as needed. Fold in the cookies.

Fill the prepared muffin tins about two-thirds full, and bake the cupcakes for about 18 minutes, or until an indentation made with your finger in the center of the cupcakes springs back. These cupcakes were designed to look pale, so don't look for a golden color from baking.

Remove the tins from the oven, allow the cupcakes to cool in the pan for 10 minutes, then transfer them to wire racks to cool completely.

For the coffee buttercream, finish the German Buttercream, then beat in the vanilla bean paste, mixing just until it's combined.

Fill a piping bag with the buttercream, and pipe a generous amount onto each cupcake. Sprinkle the tops of the cupcakes with the crushed cookies.

These Oreo® Latte Cupcakes are best served at room temperature. Store them in an airtight container in the fridge for up to a week.

COFFEE GERMAN BUTTERCREAM
1 batch of German Buttercream (page 16)

1 tsp espresso powder, whisked with the sugar and cornstarch in the base recipe

1 tsp vanilla bean paste or high-quality vanilla extract

OREO CUPCAKES
1¼ cups (145 g) cake flour, spooned and leveled

1 cup (200 g) granulated sugar

¼ tsp baking soda

½ tsp baking powder

¼ tsp salt

¼ cup (56 g) unsalted butter, room temperature

¼ cup (60 ml) canola oil

2 large egg whites, room temperature

2 tsp (10 ml) vanilla extract

⅓ cup (80 ml) whole milk, room temperature

½ cup (113 g) sour cream

5 (60 g) chocolate sandwich cookies (I use Oreo), crushed, plus more for topping

CHOCOLATE VANILLA HI-HAT CUPCAKES

Everyone loves a classic chocolate and vanilla cupcake. This recipe uses my go-to cupcake base—it's moist, fluffy, beautiful and pairs well with any kind of frosting, especially a creamy Chocolate Ermine Buttercream dunked in a dark chocolate shell.

Begin by making the custard for the Ermine Buttercream at least a few hours before frosting the cupcakes, so it has time to cool. For the cupcakes, preheat the oven to 350°F (177°C), and line 13 muffin tins with paper liners.

Place the flour, sugar, baking soda, baking powder and salt in a large bowl, and whisk them together until the mixture is well combined. Add the butter and oil, and use an electric mixer on medium speed to combine the mixture. Add the egg whites, and continue to beat the mixture until the egg whites are fully incorporated. With the mixer on medium speed, add the vanilla bean paste and sour cream, followed by the milk. Beat the mixture just until the batter is fully combined. Make sure to scrape down the sides of the bowl as needed.

Fill the prepared muffin tins about two-thirds full. Bake the cupcakes for about 20 minutes, or until an indentation made with your finger in the cupcakes springs back. These cupcakes were designed to look pale, so don't look for a golden color from baking. Remove the cupcakes from the oven, let them cool in the pan for 10 minutes, then transfer them to a cooling rack.

For the buttercream, in a small bowl, melt the chocolate chips in the microwave for 20-second intervals, stirring after each interval, until the chocolate is smooth, 1 to 2 minutes. Set it aside to cool. Finish the Ermine Buttercream, then add the cooled chocolate, cocoa powder and vanilla; mix just until they're fully combined.

Place the buttercream in a piping bag fitted with a large circle tip, and pipe it onto the cupcakes. Freeze the cupcakes for about 30 minutes, or until the buttercream is firm and does not come off the cupcake when touched.

For the Chocolate Shell, in a small bowl, melt the dark chocolate chips with the oil in the microwave for 20-second intervals, stirring after each interval, until the chocolate is smooth, 1 to 2 minutes. Dunk each chilled cupcake into the chocolate mixture, then transfer it to a platter. When all of the cupcakes have been coated, refrigerate the platter for 10 minutes to set the chocolate top.

These Chocolate Vanilla Hi-Hat Cupcakes are best served at room temperature or slightly chilled. Store them in an airtight container in the fridge for up to a week.

CHOCOLATE ERMINE BUTTERCREAM
1 batch of Ermine Buttercream (page 17)

½ cup (87 g) dark chocolate chips

½ cup (40 g) cocoa powder, spooned and leveled

½ tsp vanilla extract

VANILLA CUPCAKES
1½ cups (172 g) cake flour, spooned and leveled

1 cup (200 g) granulated sugar

¼ tsp baking soda

½ tsp baking powder

¼ tsp salt

¼ cup (56 g) unsalted butter, room temperature

¼ cup (60 ml) canola oil

2 large egg whites, room temperature

1 tsp vanilla bean paste or high-quality vanilla extract

½ cup (113 g) sour cream

⅓ cup (80 ml) whole milk, room temperature

CHOCOLATE SHELL
1 cup (175 g) dark chocolate chips

2 tsp (10 g) coconut oil

ALMOND RASPBERRY CUPCAKES

Almond may not be the first flavor that comes to mind when you think cupcakes, but it is a nice change from the classic vanilla. There's just something about almond and raspberry that goes so well together. These cupcakes are perfect for when you need a dessert that's not superheavy and intense; it's a light and fluffy cupcake topped with a silky, rich Raspberry Swiss Meringue Buttercream.

For the cupcakes, preheat the oven to 350°F (177°C) and line 13 muffin tins with paper liners.

Place the flour, sugar, baking soda, baking powder and salt in a large bowl and whisk them together until the mixture is well combined. Add the butter and oil and use an electric mixer, on medium speed, to combine the mixture. Add the egg whites and continue to beat the mixture until the egg whites are fully incorporated. Add the almond extract, milk and sour cream, beating the mixture on medium speed until the batter is fully combined. Make sure to scrape down the sides of the bowl as needed.

Fill the prepared muffin tins about two-thirds full. Bake the cupcakes for about 18 minutes, or until an indentation made with your finger in the cupcakes springs back. These cupcakes were designed to look pale, so don't look for a golden color from baking. Remove the cupcakes from the oven, let them cool in the pan for 10 minutes, then transfer them to a cooling rack to cool completely.

Make the batch of Swiss Meringue Buttercream, then beat in the raspberry preserves and lemon juice. Switch to a paddle attachment, and beat the buttercream on low speed for about 5 minutes to release any air bubbles. This will make it easier to frost the cupcakes. Fill a piping bag with the buttercream, and pipe the desired amount onto each cupcake.

These Almond Raspberry Cupcakes are best served at room temperature. Store them in an airtight container in the fridge for up to a week.

YIELD: 13 CUPCAKES

ALMOND CUPCAKE

1½ cups (172 g) cake flour, spooned and leveled

1 cup (200 g) granulated sugar

¼ tsp baking soda

½ tsp baking powder

¼ tsp salt

¼ cup (56 g) unsalted butter, room temperature

¼ cup (60 ml) canola oil

2 large egg whites, room temperature

1 tsp almond extract

⅓ cup (80 ml) whole milk, room temperature

½ cup (113 g) sour cream, room temperature

RASPBERRY SWISS MERINGUE BUTTERCREAM

1 batch of Swiss Meringue Buttercream (page 13)

½ cup (170 g) raspberry preserves (I use Bonne Maman)

2 tbsp (30 ml) lemon juice

DULCE DE LECHE CUPCAKES

When I first tried Russian Buttercream (page 18), I knew I had to make a version using dulce de leche. I love this frosting, because it complements everything, is so incredibly easy to make and still so delicious.

For the cupcakes, preheat the oven to 350°F (177°C), and line 13 muffin tins with paper liners.

Place the flour, granulated and brown sugars, baking soda, baking powder, salt, cinnamon, nutmeg, cloves and ginger in a large bowl. Whisk the ingredients together until the mixture is well combined. Add the butter and oil, and use an electric mixer on medium speed to combine the mixture. Add the egg whites, and continue to beat the mixture until the egg whites are fully incorporated. With the mixer on medium speed, add the vanilla, sour cream and milk. Beat the mixture just until the batter is fully combined. Make sure to scrape down the sides of the bowl as needed.

Fill the prepared muffin tins about two-thirds to three-quarters full, and bake the cupcakes for about 20 minutes, or until an indentation made with your finger in the cupcakes springs back. Allow them to cool in the pan for 10 minutes, then move the cupcakes to a cooling rack to cool completely. Once the cupcakes are cool, use a cupcake corer, or something of the same size, to create a hole in the center of the cupcakes. Discard the cake from the holes.

For the Cinnamon Sugar Coating, combine the sugar and cinnamon in a shallow bowl. Use a pastry brush to brush the butter onto the sides and tops of the cupcakes, then roll them in the cinnamon sugar, one at a time.

For the buttercream, make the batch of Russian Buttercream, using half a can of the dulce de leche instead of the sweetened condensed milk in the base recipe. Fill a piping bag with some of the remaining half a can of dulce de leche, and pipe the dulce de leche into the holes in the cupcakes. If there is any remaining dulce de leche after the holes are filled, mix it into the buttercream.

Fill another piping bag, fitted with your favorite piping tip, with the Dulce de Leche Russian Buttercream, and pipe a generous amount onto each cupcake.

These Dulce de Leche Cupcakes are best served slightly chilled. Store them in an airtight container in the fridge for up to a week.

YIELD: 13 CUPCAKES

CHURRO CUPCAKE
1½ cups (172 g) cake flour, spooned and leveled

½ cup (100 g) granulated sugar

½ cup (95 g) packed brown sugar

¼ tsp baking soda

½ tsp baking powder

¼ tsp salt

¾ tsp cinnamon

½ tsp nutmeg

¼ tsp cloves

¼ tsp ginger

¼ cup (56 g) unsalted butter, room temperature

¼ cup (60 ml) canola oil

2 large egg whites, room temperature

1 tsp vanilla extract

½ cup (113 g) sour cream

⅓ cup (80 ml) whole milk, room temperature

CINNAMON SUGAR COATING
½ cup (100 g) granulated sugar

1 tsp cinnamon

2 tbsp (28 g) unsalted butter, melted

DULCE DE LECHE RUSSIAN BUTTERCREAM
1 batch of Russian Buttercream (page 18), made with dulche de leche instead of sweetened condensed milk

1 (13.4-oz [380-g]) can dulce de leche (I use Nestle), divided

HAZELNUT MOCHA CUPCAKES

Chocolate pairs so well with so many flavors. Two of my favorites are coffee and hazelnut, which also happen to pair well together. So, is there anything better than a supermoist chocolate cupcake that's enriched with espresso powder and brewed coffee, filled with chocolate hazelnut spread and frosted with silky Italian Meringue Buttercream (page 14)? For good measure, I flavored the buttercream with chocolate, hazelnut and coffee.

For the cupcakes, preheat the oven to 350°F (177°C), and line 14 muffin tins with paper liners.

In a medium bowl, whisk together the flour, sugar, cocoa powder, espresso powder, salt, baking soda and baking powder.

In a large bowl, whisk together the eggs and oil until the mixture is smooth. Add the vanilla and coffee, mixing until they're well combined. Sift the dry ingredients over the wet, and whisk the mixture until it's fully combined.

Distribute the batter evenly among the prepared muffin tins. Bake the cupcakes for 16 to 17 minutes, until an indentation made with your finger in the cupcakes springs back. Remove the cupcakes from the oven, cool them in the pan for 10 minutes, then transfer them to a cooling rack to cool completely.

For the hazelnut buttercream, make the batch of Italian Meringue Buttercream, then add the espresso mixture, chocolate hazelnut spread and cocoa powder, mixing just until they're evenly distributed.

For the filling, use a cupcake corer, or something of the same size, to create a hole in the center of the cupcakes; discard the cake from the holes. Place the chocolate hazelnut spread in a piping bag, and use it to fill the holes in the cupcakes. Put the buttercream in another piping bag with your favorite tip, and pipe a generous amount onto each cupcake. Top the buttercream with the hazelnuts.

These Hazelnut Mocha Cupcakes are best served at room temperature. Store them in an airtight container in the fridge for up to a week.

YIELD: 14 CUPCAKES

CHOCOLATE CUPCAKES
1 cup (120 g) all-purpose flour, spooned and leveled

1 cup (200 g) granulated sugar

½ cup (40 g) Dutch-process cocoa powder, spooned and leveled

1 tsp espresso powder

¼ tsp salt

¼ tsp baking soda

½ tsp baking powder

2 large eggs, room temperature

½ cup (120 ml) canola oil

2 tsp (10 ml) vanilla

¾ cup (180 ml) brewed coffee, room temperature

HAZELNUT MOCHA ITALIAN MERINGUE BUTTERCREAM
1 batch of Italian Meringue Buttercream (page 14)

2 tsp (4 g) espresso powder dissolved in 1 tsp hot water and cooled

½ cup (150 g) chocolate hazelnut spread (I use Nutella)

¼ cup (20 g) unsweetened cocoa powder, spooned and leveled

FILLING
½ cup (150 g) chocolate hazelnut spread (I use Nutella)

TOPPING
Crushed hazelnuts

BANANA COOKIE BUTTER CUPCAKES

I don't know how I lived the last 25 years without ever pairing banana and cookie butter together. They're literally a match made in heaven, and the Cookie Butter Swiss Meringue Buttercream is to die for. These cupcakes are going to make you a lot of friends: even my non-dessert-loving husband ate two of them!

For the cupcakes, preheat the oven to 350°F (177°C), and line 12 muffin tins with paper liners.

In a medium bowl, whisk together the flour, baking soda, baking powder, cinnamon and salt.

In a large bowl, whisk together the granulated and brown sugars and egg until the mixture is smooth. Add the oil, Greek yogurt and vanilla, whisking until they're fully incorporated. Add the bananas to the mixture, and mix until they're fully combined. Add the dry ingredients, and mix until the flour is just barely incorporated.

Distribute the batter evenly among the prepared muffin tins, and bake the cupcakes for about 22 minutes, or until an indentation made with your finger in the cupcakes springs back. Cool the cupcakes in the pan for 10 minutes, then transfer them to a cooling rack to cool completely.

For the cookie butter buttercream, make the batch of Swiss Meringue Buttercream, then add the cookie butter and the vanilla bean paste; mix just until they're fully incorporated.

For the filling, use a cupcake corer, or something of the same size, to create a hole in the centers of the cupcakes. Discard the cake from the holes. Place the cookie butter in a piping bag, and use it to fill the holes. Put the buttercream in another piping bag with your favorite tip, and pipe a generous amount onto each cupcake.

These Banana Cookie Butter Cupcakes are best served at room temperature. Store them in an airtight container in the fridge for up to a week.

YIELD: 12 CUPCAKES

BANANA CUPCAKE
1¼ cups (150 g) all-purpose flour, spooned and leveled

¼ tsp baking soda

1 tsp baking powder

½ tsp cinnamon

¼ tsp salt

½ cup (100 g) granulated sugar

¼ cup (47 g) packed brown sugar

1 large egg, room temperature

¼ cup (60 ml) canola oil

¼ cup (56 g) Greek yogurt

1 tsp vanilla extract

2 medium ripe bananas, mashed

COOKIE BUTTER SWISS MERINGUE BUTTERCREAM
1 batch of Swiss Meringue Buttercream (page 13)

½ cup (120 g) cookie butter (I use Lotus Biscoff)

1 tsp vanilla bean paste or high-quality vanilla extract

FILLING
½ cup (120 g) cookie butter (I use Lotus Biscoff)

DOUBLE CHOCOLATE
PEPPERMINT CUPCAKES

There is no better partner to peppermint than chocolate. The superlight Peppermint Meringue Frosting in this recipe is like a marshmallow cloud and the perfect topping to a dark and rich cupcake. And, let's not forget about the White Chocolate Ganache (page 21) surprise center!

For the cupcakes, preheat the oven to 350°F (177°C), and line 14 muffin tins with paper liners.

In a medium bowl, whisk together the flour, sugar, cocoa powder, espresso powder, salt, baking soda and baking powder. Set aside the dry ingredients.

In a large bowl, whisk together the eggs and the oil until the mixture is smooth. Add the vanilla and coffee, mixing until they're well combined. Sift the dry ingredients over the wet, and whisk the mixture until it's fully combined.

Distribute the batter evenly among the prepared tins; the tins should be two-thirds to three-quarters full. Bake the cupcakes for 16 to 17 minutes, until an indentation made with your finger in the cupcakes springs back. Remove the cupcakes from the oven, allow them to cool in the pan for 10 minutes then transfer them to a cooling rack to cool completely.

Make the ganache as the cupcakes cool, then set it aside.

Once the cupcakes are completely cool, use a cupcake corer, or something of the same size, to create holes in the centers of the cupcakes. With a small spoon, fill the holes with the ganache.

For the frosting, make the one and a half batches of Meringue Frosting, then beat in the vanilla bean paste and peppermint extract, just until they're fully combined.

Use a piping bag with your favorite tip to pipe the frosting onto each cupcake. For topping, sprinkle the crushed peppermint candies on top of the frosting.

These Double Chocolate Peppermint Cupcakes are best served at room temperature. Store them in an airtight container in the fridge for two to three days.

YIELD: 14 CUPCAKES

CHOCOLATE CUPCAKES
1 cup (120 g) all-purpose flour, spooned and leveled

1 cup (200 g) granulated sugar

½ cup (40 g) Dutch-process cocoa powder, spooned and leveled

1 tsp espresso powder

¼ tsp salt

¼ tsp baking soda

½ tsp baking powder

2 large eggs, room temperature

½ cup (120 ml) canola oil

2 tsp (10 ml) vanilla extract

¾ cup (180 ml) brewed coffee, room temperature

WHITE CHOCOLATE GANACHE FILLING
1 batch of Thin White Chocolate Ganache (page 21)

PEPPERMINT MERINGUE FROSTING
1½ batches of Meringue Frosting (page 20)

½ tsp vanilla bean paste or high-quality vanilla extract

½ tsp peppermint extract

TOPPING
Crushed peppermint candies

BETTER-THAN-CLASSIC
COOKIES

I'm so excited about how this chapter turned out! When you think of frosting, I'm pretty sure your first thought is something like cakes or cupcakes. You don't typically think of cookies, but I'm here to change that. I chose some classic cookies, like shortbread and sugar cookies, and turned them into more exciting, better-than-classics.

I also included several fantastic sandwich cookie recipes in this chapter, and they're so simple to make. The trick to these magical little treats is to refrigerate them until they feel firm, so that the frosting sets on the cookie well. Then, remove them from the fridge, and let the cookies sit out just long enough so that the cream softens a little.

Cookies are so perfect for sharing! Pro tip: When you don't know what to give someone, whether it's for a birthday, holiday or housewarming, you can't go wrong with dessert. The hardest part for me will be deciding which cookies to include in this year's Christmas cookie boxes. The Gingerbread House Cookies (page 113) will make it, for sure! I was also thinking the Neapolitan s'mores (page 105), the Chocolate Caramel Macchiato Cookies (page 114) and definitely the Almond Butter Cup Macarons (page 117)!

NEAPOLITAN S'MORES
SHORTBREAD COOKIES

I first made these as regular s'mores cookies, but I really wanted to show you how to make a strawberry meringue, so they're Neapolitan s'mores cookies! The graham cracker shortbread topped with creamy Milk Chocolate Ganache (page 21) and fluffy clouds of strawberry meringue seem so innocent, but they'll get you. You'll be sitting there saying, "I'll eat just one or two of them," and, before you know it, the whole pan is gone.

For the cookies, in a medium bowl, whisk together the flour, graham cracker crumbs, cinnamon and salt. Use an electric mixer to cream the butter with the sugar and vanilla for 2 to 3 minutes, until they're light and creamy. Add the dry ingredients, and mix just until the last streak of flour is combined.

Place the cookie dough between two sheets of parchment paper. With a rolling pin, roll it out to an even thickness of about ¼ inch (6 mm). Freeze the dough until it's firm, about 30 minutes. Line two baking sheets with parchment paper.

Remove the dough from the freezer. With a 1½- to 2-inch (4- to 5-cm) round cookie cutter, cut cookies as close together as possible to limit the amount of dough wasted. Carefully transfer the cookies to the prepared baking sheet. Preheat the oven to 350°F (177°C) and freeze the cut out cookies until they're firm, about 10 minutes.

Gather up the scraps and repeat the whole process to make more cookies.

Bake the cookies for 7 minutes, just until the edges are set. Allow the cookies to cool on the pan for about 5 minutes, then transfer them to a wire rack to cool completely.

Make the Thick Milk Chocolate Ganache. Cover the ganache, and allow it to cool while you make the frosting. For the strawberry frosting, make the half batch of Meringue Frosting, then add the powdered strawberries and vanilla bean paste; mix just until they're fully combined.

To assemble the cookies, use a spoon or a piping bag to drop a dollop of the ganache onto half of the cookies and another spoon or piping bag to drop frosting on the other half of the cookies. Sandwich the two together, and refrigerate the sandwiches for 30 minutes to set.

These Neapolitan S'mores Shortbread Cookies are best served at room temperature or slightly chilled. Store them in an airtight container in the fridge for two to three days.

YIELD: 25
SANDWICH
COOKIES

GRAHAM CRACKER
SHORTBREAD
COOKIES
¾ cup (90 g) all-purpose flour, spooned and leveled

¼ cup (30 g) graham cracker crumbs

⅛ tsp cinnamon

¼ tsp salt

½ cup (113 g) unsalted butter, room temperature

¼ cup (30 g) powdered sugar, spooned and leveled

1 tsp vanilla extract

CHOCOLATE
GANACHE
½ batch of Thick Milk Chocolate Ganache (page 21)

STRAWBERRY
MERINGUE
FROSTING
½ batch of Meringue Frosting (page 20)

1.2 oz (34 g) powdered freeze-dried strawberries

½ tsp vanilla bean paste or high-quality vanilla extract

TIP:

If you can't find powdered freeze-dried strawberries, you can make your own by pulsing freeze-dried strawberries in a food processor until they are powdered.

LEMON MERINGUE
SUGAR COOKIES

If anything screams summer more than chewy sugar cookies sandwiched around sweet and tangy lemon curd and homemade vanilla meringue, let me know. Yeah, I didn't think so. These babies are a major crowd-pleaser. I'm telling you: Anything you frost with a fluffy meringue is instantly irresistible!

For the lemon curd, place the lemon zest, lemon juice, egg, egg yolk, sugar, butter and salt in a medium saucepan over medium-low heat. Whisk the mixture continuously for 5 to 10 minutes, until the curd begins to thicken and coat the back of a spoon. Remove the curd from the heat, and pour it into a heatproof bowl. Cover the surface with plastic wrap, and allow the curd to cool completely to room temperature, about 2 hours. Once it's cooled, refrigerate it.

For the cookie, in a medium bowl, whisk together the flour, baking soda and salt.

In a large bowl, combine the butter, oil, sugar, egg, vanilla and lemon zest, and mix until the mixture is completely smooth, about 1 minute. Fold in the dry ingredients just until the last streak of flour is combined. Let the batter rest while you preheat the oven to 350°F (177°C), and line a baking sheet with parchment paper.

Scoop the cookie dough with a small cookie scoop onto the prepared baking sheet, 3 to 4 inches (8 to 10 cm) apart. Bake the cookies for 8 minutes, or until the edges are set but the centers are still soft and gooey; the cookies may appear a little underbaked until they cool. Allow the cookies to cool on the pan for about 5 minutes, then move them to a cooling rack.

Make the Meringue Frosting, add the vanilla bean paste and lemon extract and mix just until they're combined.

Use a piping bag with your favorite tip to pipe a ring around the edge of half of the cookies. Fill in the rings with lemon curd, and sandwich them with the bare cookies. Refrigerate the cookies for at least 1 hour to set.

These Lemon Meringue Sugar Cookies are best served slightly chilled. Store them in an airtight container in the fridge for two to three days.

YIELD: 10 SANDWICH COOKIES

LEMON CURD
Zest of 1 large lemon

¼ cup (60 ml) freshly squeezed lemon juice

1 large egg

1 large egg yolk

¼ cup (50 g) granulated sugar

3 tbsp (42 g) unsalted butter, softened

⅛ tsp salt

LEMON SUGAR COOKIE
1½ cups (180 g) all-purpose flour, spooned and leveled

½ tsp baking soda

¼ tsp salt

¼ cup (56 g) unsalted butter, melted

¼ cup (60 ml) canola oil

1 cup (200 g) granulated sugar

1 large egg, room temperature

1 tsp vanilla extract

Zest of 1 large lemon

VANILLA TOASTED MERINGUE FROSTING
½ batch of Meringue Frosting (page 20)

1 tsp vanilla bean paste or high-quality vanilla extract

½ tsp lemon extract

RASPBERRY FUNFETTI
SUGAR COOKIES

I always say, when in doubt, add sprinkles. These are classic sugar cookies frosted with Raspberry American Meringue Buttercream and a generous dose of sprinkles. I love American Meringue Buttercream (page 12) because it's as easy as American Buttercream (page 11), but it's not quite as sweet. So, it pairs well with the sugar cookie. Make sure to use seedless jam, as jam with seeds does not pipe well.

For the cookies, in a medium bowl, whisk together the flour, baking soda and salt.

In a large bowl, use an electric mixer at high speed to beat the butter with the sugar until it's creamy. Add the egg yolk and vanilla bean paste, and beat just until they're fully incorporated. Add the dry ingredients, and mix until it's almost combined.

Place the cookie dough between two sheets of parchment paper. With a rolling pin, roll the dough to an even thickness of about ¼ inch (6 mm). Freeze the dough until it's firm, about 30 minutes. Line two baking sheets with parchment paper.

Remove the dough from the freezer. With a cookie cutter, cut out cookies as close together as possible, to limit the amount of dough wasted. Carefully transfer the cookies to one of the prepared baking sheets. Freeze the filled baking sheet for 10 to 15 minutes, until the cookies are firm.

Preheat the oven to 350°F (177°C).

Gather up the scraps and repeat the whole process to make more cookies.

Bake the cookies for 13 to 14 minutes, just until the edges are set. Allow the cookies to cool on the pan for about 5 minutes, then move them to a wire rack to cool completely.

For the buttercream, make the batch of American Meringue Buttercream. Add the jam and vanilla bean paste, mixing just until they're combined.

Use a piping bag fitted with your favorite piping tip to frost the cookies. Top the frosting with the sprinkles.

These Raspberry Funfetti Sugar Cookies are best served at room temperature. Store in an airtight container at room temperature for up to 24 hours, or refrigerated for up to a week.

FUNFETTI SUGAR COOKIES

1½ cups (180 g) all-purpose flour, spooned and leveled

½ tsp baking soda

½ tsp salt

½ cup (113 g) unsalted butter, room temperature

½ cup (100 g) granulated sugar

1 egg yolk

1 tsp vanilla bean paste or high-quality vanilla extract

RASPBERRY AMERICAN MERINGUE BUTTERCREAM

1 batch of American Meringue Buttercream (page 12)

¼ cup (80 g) seedless raspberry jam (I use Smucker's; see Tip)

1 tsp vanilla bean paste or high-quality vanilla extract

TOPPING

Rainbow sprinkles

TIP:

If you can't find seedless jam, you can push regular jam through a fine sieve to remove the seeds.

CHOCOLATE CHIP
SHORTBREAD COOKIES

How does one take a chocolate chip cookie to . . . well, something that's better than a chocolate chip cookie? Turning this classic into a not-so-classic was simple. I went with a melt-in-your-mouth chocolate chip shortbread base and sandwiched it around a beautiful glossy, Milk Chocolate Ganache (page 21). It doesn't get much better than chocolate on top of chocolate chips!

For the shortbread, use an electric mixer to cream the butter with the powdered and brown sugars, until they're light and creamy, 2 to 3 minutes. Add the flour and salt, and mix just until the last streak of flour is combined. Fold in the chocolate chips until they're evenly distributed, and place the cookie dough onto a sheet of plastic wrap. Wrap the plastic wrap around the cookie dough and roll it into a log, making it an even diameter of 1½ to 2 inches (4 to 5 cm) throughout. Refrigerate the cookie dough until it's firm, 1 to 2 hours.

Preheat the oven to 350°F (177°C), and line two baking sheets with parchment paper. Slice the cookies about ¼ inch (6 mm) thick. Arrange them, 1 inch (2.5 cm) apart on the prepared baking sheets then bake them for 8 to 10 minutes, until the edges are golden brown. Allow the cookies to cool completely to room temperature.

Make the Thick Milk Chocolate Ganache, cover it and allow it to cool completely to room temperature.

To assemble the cookies, use a piping bag with your favorite tip to frost half of the cookies with the ganache, then sandwich them with the other half. Refrigerate the cookies for at least 30 minutes to set.

These Chocolate Chip Shortbread Cookies are best served at room temperature or slightly chilled. Store them in an airtight container at room temperature for up to 48 hours or refrigerate them for up to a week.

YIELD: 20 COOKIES

CHOCOLATE CHIP
SHORTBREAD
½ cup (113 g) unsalted butter, room temperature

¼ cup (30 g) powdered sugar, spooned and leveled

¼ cup (47 g) packed brown sugar

1 cup (120 g) all-purpose flour, spooned and leveled

¼ tsp salt

⅓ cup (58 g) mini chocolate chips, finely chopped

CHOCOLATE
GANACHE
1 batch of Thick Milk Chocolate Ganache (page 21)

FROSTED

GINGERBREAD HOUSE COOKIES

As everyone knows, the holidays are for baking cookies, so we obviously need a batch of Gingerbread House Cookies. I chose American Buttercream (page 11) for these beauties because it's delicious, but also because it forms a crust when it dries. That makes it easy to store and stack the cookies. You can also try them with Cream Cheese Frosting (page 19) for a tang, American Meringue Buttercream (page 12) for a less sweet option or Ermine Buttercream (page 17) for ultra fluffiness.

For the cookies, in a medium bowl, whisk together the flour, baking soda, ginger, cinnamon and salt.

Use an electric mixer at high speed to beat the butter with the sugar and molasses until the mixture is creamy. Add the egg yolk and vanilla, and beat just until they're fully incorporated. Add the dry ingredients, and mix just until the last streak of flour is combined.

Place the cookie dough between two sheets of parchment paper. With a rolling pin, roll the dough to an even thickness of about ¼ inch (6 mm). Freeze the dough until it's firm, about 30 minutes. Line two baking sheets with parchment paper.

Remove the dough. With a house-shaped cookie cutter or a knife, cut out cookies as close together as possible, to limit the amount of dough wasted. Carefully transfer the cookies to one of the prepared baking sheets. Freeze the filled baking sheet until the cookies feel firm, about 10 minutes.

Preheat the oven to 350°F (177°C).

Gather up the dough scraps, and put them between two sheets of parchment paper. Repeat the rolling and cutting process. Transfer the cookies to the second prepared baking sheet, and freeze them for 10 minutes, until the cookies are firm.

Bake the cookies for 13 to 14 minutes, just until the edges are set. Allow the cookies to cool on the pan for about 5 minutes, then move them to a wire rack to cool completely.

For the buttercream, make the half batch of American Buttercream. Add the vanilla bean paste, and mix just until it's combined.

Use a piping bag with your favorite piping tip to frost the cookies. Before the frosting sets, top the frosting with the sprinkles.

These Gingerbread House Cookies are best served at room temperature or slightly chilled. Store in an airtight container at room temperature for up to 48 hours, or refrigerated for up to a week.

YIELD: 12—16 COOKIES

GINGERBREAD SUGAR COOKIES

1¼ cups (150 g) all-purpose flour, spooned and leveled

½ tsp baking soda

1 tsp ginger

1 tsp cinnamon

¼ tsp salt

½ cup (113 g) unsalted butter, room temperature

⅓ cup (63 g) packed brown sugar

1 tbsp (21 g) molasses

1 large egg yolk, room temperature

1 tsp vanilla extract

VANILLA BEAN AMERICAN BUTTERCREAM

½ batch of American Buttercream (page 11)

1 tsp vanilla bean paste or high-quality vanilla extract

TOPPING

Clear sprinkles

CHOCOLATE CARAMEL MACCHIATO COOKIES

Don't let the title fool you, these cookies are a little easier than you think. Basically, we're just sandwiching two chocolaty, chewy sugar cookies around the most irresistible espresso- and caramel-infused Italian Meringue Buttercream (page 14).

Begin with the Caramel Sauce so it has time to cool. Place the sugar and water in a medium, light-colored saucepan with a lid over medium heat. Allow the sugar to melt in the water but DO NOT STIR IT. Once the sugar melts completely, remove the lid and watch the sugar continue to cook, until the color begins to change. After about 10 minutes, when the sugar begins to turn an amber color, remove the pan from the stove, and stir in the cream. The mixture will bubble violently, so be careful. Stir the mixture until it's completely combined, then add the butter and stir until the caramel is smooth. Add the vanilla and salt, mixing until they're completely combined. Pour the caramel into a heatproof jar, and allow it to cool completely to room temperature.

For the cookies, in a medium bowl, whisk together the flour, cocoa powder, espresso powder, baking soda and salt.

In a large bowl, combine the butter, oil and sugar. Add the eggs and vanilla, and mix until the mixture is completely smooth. Fold in the dry ingredients just until the last streak of flour is combined.

Let the batter rest while you preheat the oven to 350°F (177°C) and line six baking sheets with parchment paper.

Scoop the cookie dough with a small cookie scoop and place the scoops 2 to 3 inches (5 to 7 cm) apart on the prepared baking sheets.

Bake the cookies for 8 minutes, or until the edges are set but the centers are still soft. Allow the cookies to cool on the pan for about 5 minutes, then move them to a cooling rack to cool completely.

(Continued)

YIELD: 18 SANDWICH COOKIES

CARAMEL SAUCE
½ cup (100 g) granulated sugar

2 tbsp (30 ml) water

¼ cup (60 ml) heavy whipping cream, room temperature

2 tbsp (28 g) unsalted butter, softened

½ tsp vanilla extract

¼ tsp salt

CHOCOLATE SUGAR COOKIES
2 cups (240 g) all-purpose flour, spooned and leveled

¾ cup (60 g) Dutch-process cocoa powder, spooned and leveled

½ tsp espresso powder

¾ tsp baking soda

½ tsp salt

½ cup (113 g) unsalted butter, melted

⅓ cup (80 ml) canola oil

2 cups (400 g) granulated sugar

2 large eggs, room temperature

1 tsp vanilla extract

ALMOND BUTTER CUP MACARONS
(Continued)

Bake one sheet of macarons at a time, on the middle rack, for 14 minutes, or until their feet are fully set and they no longer look wet. Remove the baking sheet from the oven and bake the second batch. Allow the cookie shells to cool on the baking sheets until they're completely cooled.

For the buttercream, make the half batch of French Buttercream while the macarons cool. Add the almond butter and vanilla bean paste, mixing just until they're combined.

Use a piping bag fitted with your favorite tip to frost half of the cookies. Sandwich them with the other half, and refrigerate them for at least 4 hours, preferably overnight.

These Almond Butter Cup Macarons are best served slightly chilled, 24 hours after making them. Store them in an airtight container in the fridge for up to a week.

½ batch of French Buttercream (page 15)

¼ cup (63 g) almond butter (I use Justin's Vanilla Almond Butter)

1 tsp vanilla bean paste or high-quality vanilla extract

BROWNIES, BARS AND
EVERYTHING IN BETWEEN

Brownies and bars are basically gooey squares of deliciousness. This chapter includes lots of chocolaty goodness and other indulgent square-shaped treats, including no-bake Lemon Meringue Cheesecake Bars (page 125), aka your new summer guilty pleasure.

You'll notice that a lot of these recipes include many layers. Sometimes, they even look like chocolate caramel lasagna: I see you Millionaire Brownie Bars (page 123). That's because I think brownies and bars look so much tastier and more beautiful when they have multiple layers.

Honestly, this chapter has so many great recipes, I don't think I could pick a favorite. If you haven't tried white chocolate with chai (page 141), then what are you waiting for? The tiramisu (page 134) and cookie dough (page 142) brownies are going to make you a lot of friends. And, if you thought brownies were good, you're in serious need of White Chocolate Brownies (page 137).

The recipes in this chapter are so great for get-togethers. Most of them are fairly quick and easy to make, and the best part is you just have to slice them into little squares for serving. This means you can sneak one for yourself; no one will even notice!

MILLIONAIRE BROWNIE BARS

Everyone loves a classic millionaire bar, but do you know what's even better? A dark chocolate Millionaire Brownie Bar! A shortbread crust, a fudgy brownie center, a creamy salted caramel sauce and a dark chocolate ganache topping play together like it's nobody's business. Let's just say, this is not a dessert that I'm willing to share. #sorrynotsorry!

For the shortbread, grease an 8 x 8–inch (20 x 20–cm) baking pan with baking spray, and line it with parchment paper, leaving an overhang of paper above the top of the pan to easily remove the brownies.

In a small bowl, whisk together the flour, baking powder and salt.

In a large bowl, use an electric mixer to cream the butter with the sugar for 1 to 2 minutes. Add the dry ingredients, and mix until a dough is formed. Press the dough with your fingers into the prepared pan, creating an even layer on the bottom. Refrigerate the shortbread while you make the brownie layer.

For the brownies, preheat the oven to 325°F (163°C).

In a small bowl, melt the butter and the chocolate chips for 20-second intervals in the microwave, stirring after each interval, until the mixture is smooth, 1 to 2 minutes. Set aside the mixture to cool for a minute.

In another small bowl, whisk together the flour, cocoa powder and salt; set aside the bowl.

In a large bowl, whisk together the eggs and granulated and brown sugars, for just 10 to 15 seconds, until they're just barely combined. Don't overmix. Add the butter mixture, and whisk just until the mixture is fully combined; don't overmix. Add the dry ingredients, and mix just until the last streak of flour is combined.

Pour the brownie batter over the shortbread crust. Bake the brownies for about 30 minutes, until the center of the brownies look set. Remove the pan from the oven, and let the brownies cool completely to room temperature.

(Continued)

SHORTBREAD
1 cup (120 g) all-purpose flour, spooned and leveled

1 tsp baking powder

½ tsp salt

½ cup (113 g) unsalted butter, room temperature

¼ cup (30 g) powdered sugar, spooned and leveled

BROWNIE
6 tbsp (84 g) unsalted butter, softened

½ cup (87 g) semisweet chocolate chips

½ cup (60 g) all-purpose flour, spooned and leveled

2 tbsp (10 g) Dutch-process cocoa powder, spooned and leveled

¼ tsp salt

2 large eggs, room temperature

½ cup (100 g) granulated sugar

¼ cup (47 g) packed brown sugar

For the caramel sauce, place the sugar and water in a medium, light-colored saucepan with a lid over medium heat. Allow the sugar to melt in the water but DO NOT STIR IT. Once the sugar melts completely, remove the lid and watch the sugar continue to cook until the color begins to change. After about 10 minutes, when the color of the sugar turns to a light amber, remove the pan from the stove, and slowly stir in the cream. The mixture will bubble violently, so be careful. Stir the mixture until it's completely combined, then add the butter and stir until the caramel is smooth. Add the vanilla bean paste and salt, mixing until they're completely combined.

Pour the caramel sauce over the brownies, and allow the caramel to cool for about 1 hour, until the caramel is no longer hot. Refrigerate the pan until the caramel is fully set, about 2 hours.

Make the ganache and spread it on top of the chilled caramel. Sprinkle the sea salt flakes over the ganache, and freeze the brownies for 3 to 4 hours, or overnight.

Use the overhanging parchment paper to lift the brownies from the pan. With a large knife, warmed with hot water, cut the brownies into even squares.

These Millionaire Brownie Bars are best served slightly chilled. Store them in an airtight container in the fridge for up to a week.

SALTED CARAMEL SAUCE
1 cup (200 g) granulated sugar

¼ cup (60 ml) water

½ cup (120 ml) heavy whipping cream, room temperature

¼ cup (56 g) unsalted butter, softened

½ tsp vanilla bean paste or high-quality vanilla extract

½ tsp salt

DARK CHOCOLATE GANACHE
1 batch of Thick Dark Chocolate Ganache (page 21)

Pinch of sea salt flakes

LEMON MERINGUE CHEESECAKE BARS

When life gives you lemons, you make these, because anything else would be a waste of good lemons. All the rest of my lemon recipes are a good idea, too, but this recipe is my #1 lemon pick by far. I think I might have a serious obsession with toasted meringue, and I'm OK with that!

For the lemon curd, place the lemon zest, lemon juice, egg, egg yolk, sugar, butter and salt in a medium saucepan over medium-low heat. Whisk the mixture continuously for 5 to 10 minutes, until the curd begins to thicken and coat the back of a spoon. Remove the curd from the heat, and pour it into a heatproof bowl. Cover the surface with plastic wrap, and allow the curd to cool completely to room temperature, about 2 hours. Once it's cooled, refrigerate it.

For the crust, line an 8 x 8–inch (20 x 20–cm) baking pan with parchment paper, leaving an overhang of paper above the top of the pan to easily remove the bars.

Place the graham crackers in a food processor, and pulse until they're completely crushed, 1 to 2 minutes. Add the butter and pulse for a few seconds, until the butter is evenly distributed. Pour the crust into the prepared pan, and press it firmly against the bottom of the pan. Freeze the crust for at least 20 minutes.

For the filling, in a medium bowl, use an electric mixer to beat the cream until stiff peaks form, 1 to 2 minutes. Set aside the cream.

In a large bowl, use an electric mixer to beat the cream cheese and butter until they're creamy, 2 to 3 minutes. Add the sugar, and beat the mixture for 5 minutes at high speed, scraping down the sides of the bowl halfway through. Add the lemon zest, lemon juice, vanilla bean paste and salt, and beat just until they're fully incorporated. Fold in the whipped cream, being careful not to knock out all the air.

Spread the cheesecake mixture evenly over the crust, then spread the cooled lemon curd on top of the cheesecake. Tightly cover the lemon bars with plastic wrap and freeze them overnight.

(Continued)

YIELD: 16 BARS

LEMON CURD
Zest of 1 large lemon

¼ cup (60 ml) freshly squeezed lemon juice

1 large egg

1 large egg yolk

¼ cup (50 g) granulated sugar

3 tbsp (42 g) unsalted butter, softened

⅛ tsp salt

GRAHAM CRACKER CRUST
1 sleeve (300 g) honey graham crackers

¼ cup (60 g) unsalted butter, melted

LEMON CHEESECAKE FILLING
½ cup (120 ml) heavy whipping cream, cold

1 cup (227 g) cream cheese, room temperature

¼ cup (56 g) unsalted butter, room temperature

1½ cups (180 g) powdered sugar, spooned and leveled

Zest of 1 small lemon

2 tbsp (30 ml) lemon juice

1 tsp vanilla bean paste or high-quality vanilla extract

¼ tsp salt

Make the Meringue Frosting and add the vanilla bean paste, mixing just until it's fully incorporated. Spread the meringue on top of the cheesecake and use a kitchen torch or a lighter to toast the top.

Use the overhanging parchment paper to remove the cheesecake from the pan. Run a large serrated knife under hot water, then use it to cut the cheesecake into bars.

These Lemon Meringue Cheesecake Bars are best served chilled. Store them in an airtight container in the fridge for two to three days.

TOASTED VANILLA MERINGUE FROSTING

1 batch of Meringue Frosting (page 20)

½ tsp vanilla bean paste or high-quality vanilla extract

STRAWBERRIES 'N' CREAM
BLONDIE BARS

I think we can all admit that strawberries 'n' cream is just heavenly. The tang of the cream cheese is the perfect complement to a buttery, chewy blondie and fresh, sweet strawberries. The layers of strawberries between the cream cheese frosting are as visually stunning as they taste!

For the blondie, preheat the oven to 350°F (177°C). Grease an 8 x 8-inch (20 x 20-cm) baking pan with baking spray, and line it with parchment paper, leaving an overhang of paper above the top of the pan to easily remove the bars.

In a medium bowl, whisk together the butter and sugar. Add the egg and vanilla, mixing until they're fully combined. Fold in the flour and salt just until the last streak of flour is incorporated.

Spread the dough evenly in the prepared pan. Bake the blondie for 30 minutes, or until the edges are set but the center is still a little soft. Remove the pan from the oven, and allow the blondie to cool completely to room temperature.

For the frosting, thinly slice the strawberries. Place them on a paper towel, and cover them with another sheet of paper towel to soak up any excess liquid.

When the blondie is cooled, make one batch of Cream Cheese Frosting, using a total of 2 cups (240 g) of powdered sugar. Add the cream and vanilla bean paste, and beat the frosting for 2 minutes.

Spread one-third of the frosting over the blondies in the pan, then spread half of the strawberries on the frosting. Spread another one-third of the frosting on the berries, then layer the remaining berries on the frosting. Top the berries with the remaining one-third of the frosting. Refrigerate the blondies for at least 4 hours, preferably overnight.

Use the overhanging parchment paper to lift the blondies from the pan. Run a large serrated knife under hot water and use it to slice the blondies into squares.

These Strawberries 'n' Cream Blondie Bars are best served slightly chilled. Store them in an airtight container in the fridge for two to three days.

YIELD: 16
BLONDIES

BLONDIES
½ cup (113 g) unsalted butter, melted

¾ cup (150 g) granulated sugar

1 large egg, room temperature

1 tsp vanilla extract

1 cup (120 g) all-purpose flour, spooned and leveled

¼ tsp salt

STRAWBERRY CREAM CHEESE FROSTING
10 large strawberries

1 batch of Cream Cheese Frosting (page 19), minus 1 cup (120 g) of powdered sugar

2 tbsp (30 ml) heavy whipping cream, cold

2 tsp (8 g) vanilla bean paste or high-quality vanilla extract

TIRAMISU BROWNIES

Ooh, tiramisu brownies. I can't believe I didn't create this recipe sooner, but I'll definitely be making it more often. I love a good chocolate-coffee combo. And, let's not even talk about the whipped vanilla Diplomat Cream (page 23) with mascarpone! This is a great twist on the classic . . . both the classic brownie and the classic tiramisu.

Begin by making the custard for the Diplomat Cream at least a few hours before frosting the brownies, so it has time to cool.

For the brownies, preheat the oven to 325°F (163°C). Grease a 9 x 13 x 2–inch (33 x 23 x 5–cm) baking pan with baking spray, and line it with parchment paper, leaving an overhang of paper above the top of the pan to easily remove the brownies.

In a small bowl, melt the butter and the chocolate chips for 20-second intervals in the microwave, stirring after each interval, until the mixture is smooth, 1 to 2 minutes. Set aside the butter mixture to cool for a minute. In another small bowl, whisk together the flour, cocoa powder, salt and espresso powder.

In a large bowl, whisk together the eggs and granulated and brown sugars, for just 10 to 15 seconds, until they're just barely combined. Don't overmix. Add the butter mixture, whisking just until the mixture is fully combined; don't overmix. Add the dry ingredients, and mix just until the last streak of flour is combined.

Pour the brownie batter into the prepared pan. Bake the brownies for about 30 minutes, until the center of the brownies look set. Remove the pan from the oven, and allow the brownies to cool completely to room temperature.

Finish the Diplomat Cream, adding the mascarpone with the custard and stabilized whipped cream, then beat until they're fully combined and fluffy. Add the vanilla bean paste, and mix just until it's fully incorporated.

For the filling, spread a very thin layer of the cream on top of the cooled brownies, just enough to help the ladyfingers stick. Dip the ladyfingers in the coffee for about 3 seconds each, and place them in a tight line on top of the cream. Spread the rest of the cream on top of the ladyfingers, then dust the cream with the cocoa powder.

Refrigerate the Tiramisu Brownies for at least 4 hours, preferably overnight. Use the overhanging parchment paper to lift the brownies from the pan, then cut them with a large knife into squares.

These Tiramisu Brownies are best served slightly chilled. Store them in an airtight container in the fridge for up to a week.

YIELD: 24 BROWNIES

VANILLA MASCARPONE DIPLOMAT CREAM
1 batch of Diplomat Cream (page 23)

1 cup (227 g) mascarpone, room temperature

1 tsp vanilla bean paste or high-quality vanilla extract

Cocoa powder, for dusting

BROWNIES
¾ cup (170 g) unsalted butter, softened

1 cup (175 g) semisweet chocolate chips

1 cup (120 g) all-purpose flour, spooned and leveled

¼ cup (20 g) Dutch-process cocoa powder, spooned and leveled

½ tsp salt

1 tsp espresso powder

4 large eggs, room temperature

1 cup (200 g) granulated sugar

½ cup (95 g) packed brown sugar

FILLING
1 (7-oz [200-g]) package ladyfingers

1½ cups (360 ml) strong brewed coffee or cold brew, room temperature

WHITE CHOCOLATE BROWNIES

Don't let the name fool you, these babies are not brown at all . . . but people do use the name brownies for a variety of other flavors of brownies. No matter what you call them, these white chocolate bars are delicious!

For the brownies, preheat the oven to 325°F (163°C). Grease an 8 x 8–inch (20 x 20–cm) baking pan with baking spray, and line it with parchment paper, leaving an overhang of paper above the top of the pan to easily remove the brownies.

In a large bowl, melt the white chocolate chips in the microwave for 15-second intervals, stirring after each interval, until smooth, about 1 minute. Add the butter, and mix until the butter melts. Whisk in the sugar, eggs, egg yolks and vanilla, just until the mixture is combined. Fold in the flour and salt, just until the last streak of flour is combined.

Spread the mixture evenly into the prepared pan, and bake the brownies for 40 to 45 minutes, until the center feels set and the edges are golden brown. Remove the pan from the oven, and let the brownies cool completely in the pan to room temperature.

Make one batch of the Thick White Chocolate Ganache, then whip the ganache as directed on page 21. Add the cookies, vanilla bean paste and salt to the whipped chocolate, and beat for 1 minute.

Spread the ganache on the cooled brownies, and top it with extra cookie crumbs. Refrigerate the brownies for 15 minutes to set the ganache.

Use the overhanging parchment paper to lift the brownies from the pan. Cut the brownies into even squares.

The White Chocolate Brownies are best served at room temperature. Store them in an airtight container at room temperature for up to 48 hours, or refrigerated for up to a week.

WHITE CHOCOLATE BROWNIES

1 cup (175 g) white chocolate chips

¾ cup (170 g) unsalted butter, softened

¾ cup (150 g) granulated sugar

2 large eggs, room temperature

2 large egg yolks, room temperature

1 tsp vanilla extract

1 cup (120 g) all-purpose flour, spooned and leveled

¼ tsp salt

WHITE CHOCOLATE GANACHE

1 batch of Thick White Chocolate Ganache (page 21)

3 chocolate sandwich cookies, crushed (I use Oreo), plus more for garnish, optional

½ tsp vanilla bean paste or high-quality vanilla extract

⅛ tsp salt

BROWNIES, BARS AND EVERYTHING IN BETWEEN

GERMAN CHOCOLATE
BROWNIE BARS

These fancy little babies are topped with a creamy coconut and pecan custard. As if that wasn't enough, there's also a layer of silky Dark Chocolate Ganache (page 21) topped with a generous pinch of sea salt flakes.

For the brownies, preheat the oven to 325°F (163°C). Grease a 9 x 13 x 2-inch (33 x 23 x 5-cm) baking pan with baking spray, and line it with parchment paper, leaving an overhang of paper above the top of the pan to easily remove the brownies.

In a small bowl, melt the butter and the chocolate for 20-second intervals in the microwave, stirring after each interval, until the mixture is smooth, 1 to 2 minutes. Set aside the mixture to cool for a minute. In another small bowl, whisk together the flour, cocoa powder and salt.

In a large bowl, whisk together the eggs and granulated and brown sugars, for just 10 to 15 seconds, until they're just barely combined. Don't overmix. Add the butter mixture, whisking just until the mixture is fully combined; don't overmix. Add the dry ingredients, and mix just until the last streak of flour is combined.

Pour the brownie batter into the prepared pan, and bake the brownies for about 30 minutes, until the center of the brownies looks set. Remove the pan from the oven, and allow the brownies to cool in the pan.

For the filling, in a medium saucepan, combine the cream, brown sugar, egg yolks, butter and salt. Cook the mixture over medium-low heat, whisking continuously. Once the mixture is thick enough to coat the back of a spoon, 5 to 10 minutes, remove it from the heat. Stir in the vanilla bean paste, pecans and coconut. Pour the mixture over the brownies, and refrigerate them for 1 to 2 hours.

While the brownies chill, make the Thick Dark Chocolate Ganache. Pour the ganache over the coconut pecan filling. Refrigerate the brownies for at least 2 hours, until the ganache is fully set.

Sprinkle sea salt flakes over the ganache. Use the overhanging parchment paper to lift the bars from the pan. Run a large serrated knife under hot water and use it to slice the bars.

German Chocolate Brownie Bars are best served at room temperature or slightly chilled. Store them in an airtight container in the fridge for up to a week.

YIELD: 36 BARS

BROWNIES
¾ cup (170 g) unsalted butter, softened

1 cup (175 g) semisweet chocolate

1 cup (120 g) all-purpose flour, spooned and leveled

¼ cup (20 g) Dutch-process cocoa powder, spooned and leveled

½ tsp salt

4 large eggs, room temperature

1 cup (200 g) granulated sugar

½ cup (95 g) packed brown sugar

COCONUT PECAN FILLING
½ cup (120 ml) heavy whipping cream

1 cup (190 g) packed brown sugar

2 egg yolks

¼ cup (56 g) unsalted butter, softened

¼ tsp salt

1 tsp vanilla bean paste or high-quality vanilla extract

½ cup (55 g) chopped pecans

¾ cup (60 g) unsweetened shredded coconut

DARK CHOCOLATE GANACHE
1½ batches of Thick Dark Chocolate Ganache (page 21)

Pinch of sea salt flakes

WHITE CHOCOLATE CHAI
COOKIE BARS

Chai is like coffee; it's an acquired taste. If you've never had it, it may take some time to get used to. But, if you like it, you most certainly understand why I have a handful of chai recipes in this book. These cookie bars, paired with a luscious White Chocolate Russian Buttercream, are easy to make and even easier to eat. They're the perfect holiday treat!

For the bars, preheat the oven to 350°F (177°C). Grease an 8 x 8–inch (20 x 20–cm) baking pan with baking spray, and line it with parchment paper, leaving an overhang of paper above the top of the pan to easily remove the cookie bars.

In a medium bowl, whisk together the flour, baking soda, salt, cinnamon, cardamom, nutmeg, cloves, ginger, allspice and pepper.

In a large bowl, whisk together the butter and brown and granulated sugars, until they're well combined. Add the egg and mix the ingredients together until the mixture is smooth. Use a spatula to fold in the dry ingredients until everything is fully combined into a thick dough.

Spread the dough evenly in the prepared baking pan. Bake the bars for 23 minutes, or until the edges are set and the center feels a little soft. Remove the pan from the oven, and allow the bars to cool completely in the pan.

To make the buttercream, melt the white chocolate chips in a small bowl in the microwave for 15-second intervals, stirring after each interval, until it's smooth, about 1 minute. Cover the bowl and set it aside to cool the chocolate to room temperature.

Make the half batch of Russian Buttercream. Add the cooled white chocolate and vanilla bean paste, and mix until they're incorporated.

Spread the buttercream evenly over the cookie bars, and refrigerate them for 15 minutes to set the frosting.

Use the overhanging parchment paper to lift the bars from the pan, then cut them into even triangles or squares, your preference!

These White Chocolate Chai Cookie Bars are best served slightly chilled or at room temperature. Store them in an airtight container at room temperature for up to 48 hours, or refrigerated for up to a week.

YIELD: 16 BARS

CHAI COOKIE BARS

1½ cups (180 g) all-purpose flour, spooned and leveled

½ tsp baking soda

¼ tsp salt

1 tsp cinnamon

½ tsp cardamom

½ tsp nutmeg

½ tsp cloves

½ tsp ginger

¼ tsp allspice

Pinch of black pepper

½ cup (113 g) unsalted butter, melted

½ cup (95 g) packed brown sugar

½ cup (100 g) granulated sugar

1 large egg, room temperature

WHITE CHOCOLATE RUSSIAN BUTTERCREAM

½ cup (87 g) white chocolate chips

½ batch of Russian Buttercream (page 18)

1 tsp vanilla bean paste or high-quality vanilla extract

COOKIE DOUGH BROWNIE BARS

Once upon a time I had a brilliant idea to sandwich two brownies around cookie dough frosting. Apparently, everyone had the same brilliant idea around the same time, because they've become increasingly popular recently. I chose Ermine Buttercream (page 17) for this frosting, because it's already got flour and milk in it, and I substituted the granulated sugar for brown sugar to better resemble cookie dough!

For the frosting filling, make the custard for the Ermine Buttercream, using brown sugar instead of granulated sugar, at least a few hours before frosting the brownies to give it time to cool.

For the brownies, preheat the oven to 325°F (163°C). Grease two 8 x 8–inch (20 x 20–cm) baking pans with baking spray, and line them with parchment paper, leaving an overhang of paper above the top of the pans to easily remove the brownies.

In a small bowl, melt the butter and the chocolate chips for 20-second intervals in the microwave, stirring after each interval, until the mixture is smooth, 1 to 2 minutes. Set aside the mixture to cool for a minute.

In another small bowl, whisk together the flour, cocoa powder, salt and espresso powder.

In a large bowl, whisk together the eggs, granulated and brown sugars and vanilla, for 10 to 15 seconds, until they're just barely combined. Don't overmix. Add the butter mixture, whisking just until the mixture is fully combined; don't overmix. Add the dry ingredients, and mix just until the last streak of flour is combined.

Distribute the brownie batter evenly into the prepared pans, and bake the brownies for about 20 minutes, until the center of the brownies looks set. Remove the pans from the oven, allow the brownies to cool for 30 minutes, then refrigerate them.

Finish the Ermine Buttercream. Add the vanilla bean paste and chocolate chips, and mix until they're evenly distributed.

Spread the buttercream on top of one of the brownies. Remove the other brownie from the pan, place it on top of the Ermine Buttercream, then press down firmly. Refrigerate the brownies for at least 4 hours, preferably overnight.

Use the overhanging parchment paper to lift the brownies from the pan. With a large serrated knife, heated with hot water, cut the brownies into squares.

These Cookie Dough Brownie Bars are best served slightly chilled or at room temperature. Store them in an airtight container in the fridge for up to a week.

YIELD: 16 BARS

COOKIE DOUGH FROSTING FILLING
½ batch of Ermine Buttercream (page 17), use brown sugar instead of granulated sugar

1 tsp vanilla bean paste or high-quality vanilla extract

1 cup (175 g) mini chocolate chips, chopped

BROWNIES
¾ cup (170 g) unsalted butter, softened

1 cup (175 g) semisweet chocolate chips

1 cup (120 g) all-purpose flour, spooned and leveled

¼ cup (20 g) Dutch-process cocoa powder, spooned and leveled

½ tsp salt

½ tsp espresso powder

4 large eggs, room temperature

1 cup (200 g) granulated sugar

½ cup (95 g) packed dark brown sugar

1 tsp vanilla extract

FROSTED

142

DESSERT FOR BREAKFAST

Dessert for breakfast is never a bad idea! These treats are perfect for any occasion, whether it's Christmas morning, brunch with the girls or you've decided to declare a personal Treat Yo' Self Day (name that line, too, and we're best friends).

There are so many great treats in this book, but the ones in this chapter are among my favorites. I just simply can't resist anything made with a sweet dough, pumpkin or cinnamon. I know you're going to love this chapter as much as I do, because who doesn't love to eat frosting for breakfast? You're welcome.

The Bundt cake (page 148) has a spiced pumpkin crumb and a cinnamon sugar swirl that is to die for. Let's not even talk about the peach donuts (page 155). They're spiced, covered in cinnamon sugar, frosted with the fluffiest white chocolate buttercream and topped with sweet peaches. Clearly, I love cinnamon sugar. I'm pretty sure it's my weapon of choice when it comes to baking. I've yet to taste something smothered in cinnamon sugar that is anything short of amazing.

I had so much fun baking up all of these delicious breakfast desserts. Wouldn't it be wonderful if I could have all of you over for brunch one day? But since I can't, think of the recipes in this chapter as me serving you brunch!

PULL-APART MAPLE APPLE BREAD

Let's start this chapter off strong, with a gooey pull-apart bread stuffed with apples, butter, cinnamon and sugar and topped with the creamiest Maple Cream Cheese Frosting. Make this bread irresistible by frosting it while it's still warm.

For the dough, grease a 9 x 5 x 3–inch (23 x 13 x 6–cm) loaf pan and line it with parchment paper. In a small bowl, stir together the milk, yeast and half of the sugar. Let the mixture rest for 10 minutes, until the top turns foamy.

Place the flour, the remaining sugar and the salt in the bowl of a stand mixer fitted with the hook attachment. Turn the mixer to low speed, add the egg and egg yolk, followed by the milk mixture and the butter. Turn the mixer to medium-low speed and knead the dough for 10 minutes, or until it begins to peel itself away from the sides of the bowl and forms a ball around the hook attachment. If this doesn't happen after 15 minutes, the dough is too sticky; add 2 tablespoons (14 g) of flour and continue to knead until the dough comes together. Move the dough to one side of the bowl, grease the open side, then repeat with the other side. Cover the bowl with plastic wrap and place it in a warm environment, such as in the sunlight or on a stovetop warming zone. Allow it to proof until it's doubled in size, about 1 hour.

For the Apple Filling, on a well-floured surface, use a rolling pin to roll the dough into an even square about ¼ inch (6 mm) thick. Spread the butter onto the dough, and top it with the sugar and cinnamon. Slice the dough into 16 even squares. Place a couple slices of apple on each square of dough and gently stack the squares, a few at a time. Place the stacks, upright, into the prepared pan. Allow the dough to rest in the pan while you preheat the oven to 325°F (163°C).

Bake the bread for 30 minutes, then increase the oven temperature to 350°F (177°C). Bake the bread for 25 minutes, or until the bread is a little darker than golden brown. Allow the bread to cool in the pan for 15 to 20 minutes.

For the Maple Cream Cheese Frosting, make the half batch of Cream Cheese Frosting. Add the vanilla bean paste, maple syrup and the cream, and mix until they're fully combined. Remove the bread from the pan and, while it's still warm, spread the frosting on top. This Pull-Apart Maple Apple Bread is best served fresh and warm. Store it in an airtight container at room temperature for up to 24 hours, or refrigerate it for two to three days.

TIP:
If you don't have a stand mixer, you can use your hands to combine the dough and to knead it. The dough is ready for proofing when you stretch it between your fingers and it's thin enough to see light through it without it ripping.

YIELD: 12 SERVINGS

DOUGH
1 cup (240 ml) milk, warmed to 120°F (49°C)

2¼ tsp (7 g) active dry yeast

¼ cup (50 g) granulated sugar, divided

3½ cups (420 g) all-purpose flour, spooned and leveled, plus more if needed

½ tsp salt

1 large egg, room temperature

1 large egg yolk, room temperature

½ cup (113 g) unsalted butter, softened

APPLE FILLING
2 tbsp (28 g) unsalted butter, softened

⅓ cup (63 g) packed brown sugar

1 tsp cinnamon

3 medium apples, thinly sliced

MAPLE CREAM CHEESE FROSTING
½ batch of Cream Cheese Frosting (page 19)

½ tsp vanilla bean paste or high-quality vanilla extract

¼ cup (60 ml) maple syrup

2 tbsp (30 ml) heavy whipping cream

RUMCHATA PUMPKIN BUNDT CAKE

It's the middle of summer and I'm over here enjoying a large slice of pumpkin Bundt cake with my vanilla latte like it's nobody's business. I know you want pumpkin cake in the summer, too, especially if there's Rumchata frosting involved. This German Buttercream (page 16), infused with the perfect dose of Rumchata, is pretty addicting!

Begin by making the custard for the German Buttercream at least a few hours before frosting the cake, so it has time to cool.

For the Cinnamon Swirl, in a medium bowl, combine the pecans, sugar, cinnamon and salt. Set aside the bowl.

For the cake, preheat the oven to 350°F (177°C), and grease a Bundt pan with baking spray.

In a medium bowl, whisk together the flour, baking soda, baking powder, salt, cinnamon, nutmeg, cloves and ginger.

In a large bowl, whisk together the eggs, granulated and brown sugars, oil, pumpkin and vanilla until the mixture is completely smooth, about 1 minute. Add the dry ingredients to the wet, and whisk the mixture just until the last streak of flour is combined.

Pour one-third of the batter into the prepared pan, then top it with half of the cinnamon filling. Make a second layer with one-third of the batter and the remaining half of the cinnamon filling. Top the filling with the last one-third of the batter.

Bake the Bundt cake for 50 to 55 minutes, until the tallest point springs back when you make an indentation on it with your finger. Cool the cake in the pan for 30 minutes, invert it onto a cooling rack and let it cool completely.

For the Rumchata buttercream, finish the German Buttercream. Then, add the Rumchata and vanilla bean paste, and mix just until they're fully incorporated.

Frost the chilled cake with the rumchata buttercream.

This Rumchata Pumpkin Bundt Cake is best served at room temperature. Store it in an airtight container in the fridge for up to a week.

FROSTED

YIELD: 12 SLICES

RUMCHATA GERMAN BUTTERCREAM
1 batch of German Buttercream (page 16)

2 tbsp (30 ml) Rumchata

1 tsp vanilla bean paste or high-quality vanilla extract

CINNAMON SWIRL
½ cup (50 g) pecans, chopped

½ cup (95 g) packed brown sugar

2 tsp (4 g) cinnamon

⅛ tsp salt

PUMPKIN BUNDT CAKE
3 cups (360 g) all-purpose flour, spooned and leveled

1 tsp baking soda

2 tsp (10 g) baking powder

½ tsp salt

2 tsp (4 g) cinnamon

1 tsp nutmeg

1 tsp cloves

1 tsp ginger

4 large eggs, room temperature

1 cup (200 g) granulated sugar

1 cup (195 g) packed brown sugar

1 cup (240 ml) canola oil

1 (15-oz [425-g]) can pumpkin puree

2 tsp (10 ml) vanilla extract

BUTTERSCOTCH BANANA BREAD

I'm a sucker for banana bread in general, but when you add butterscotch chips and a sweet frosting infused with melted butterscotch, there's no topping that. A fun way to change this banana bread up a little is to use different kinds of chocolate chips inside the bread and in the frosting. White chocolate, milk chocolate, dark chocolate, you name it!

YIELD: 10 SLICES

BANANA BREAD
1½ cups (180 g) all-purpose flour, spooned and leveled

1 tsp baking soda

½ tsp cinnamon

¼ tsp salt

½ cup (120 ml) canola oil

2 large eggs, room temperature

1 cup (190 g) packed brown sugar

1 tsp vanilla extract

1 cup (150 g, 2 large) bananas, mashed

1 cup (175 g) butterscotch chips

BUTTERSCOTCH AMERICAN BUTTERCREAM
¼ cup (44 g) butterscotch chips

½ batch of American Buttercream (page 11)

1 tsp vanilla bean paste or high-quality vanilla extract

For the bread, preheat the oven to 350°F (177°C). Grease a 9 x 5 x 3–inch (23 x 13 x 6–cm) loaf pan with baking spray and line it with parchment paper.

In a medium bowl, whisk together the flour, baking soda, cinnamon and salt. Remove and reserve 1 tablespoon (7 g) of the mixture, then set aside the rest of the dry ingredients.

In a large bowl, whisk together the oil, eggs, sugar and vanilla until the mixture is smooth. Add the bananas to the mixture, and mix until they're fully combined. Add the dry ingredients, and mix until the flour is just barely incorporated. In a small bowl, toss the butterscotch chips with the reserved flour mixture, then fold them into the batter until they're evenly distributed.

Bake the bread for 50 to 60 minutes, until the center springs back when you make an indentation in it with your finger. Allow the banana bread to cool in the pan for 30 minutes, then move it onto a cooling rack to cool completely to room temperature.

For the butterscotch buttercream, in a small bowl, melt the butterscotch chips in the microwave for 15-second intervals, stirring after each interval, until they're smooth, about 1 minute. Set aside the butterscotch to cool while you make the half batch of American Buttercream. Add the cooled butterscotch and vanilla bean paste, mixing just until they're fully incorporated.

Spread the butterscotch frosting over the banana bread. Refrigerate the bread for about 20 minutes before slicing it.

This Butterscotch Banana Bread is best served at room temperature. Store it in an airtight container in the fridge for up to a week.

CHOCOLATE LOVER'S BROWNIE BREAD

When you can't decide between a quick bread or a brownie, breakfast or dessert, delicious or delicious, always choose brownie bread. My goal was to make a rich chocolate loaf, and when it accidentally turned out like a brownie, I was all about it. Embracing the accident, I topped this beauty with a generous amount of silky, dark chocolate Russian Buttercream (page 18)! Can we say chocolate lover's dream?

For the bread, preheat the oven to 350°F (177°C). Grease a 9 x 5 x 3–inch (23 x 13 x 6–cm) loaf pan, and line it with parchment paper.

In a small bowl, melt the chocolate chips in the microwave for 20-second intervals, stirring after each interval, until the chocolate is smooth, 1 to 2 minutes. Set aside the bowl.

In another small bowl, whisk together the flour, cocoa powder, baking soda, baking powder and salt. Remove and reserve 1 tablespoon (7 g) of the mixture, then set aside the rest of the dry ingredients.

In a large bowl, whisk together the butter, eggs and sugar until they're smooth. Add the Greek yogurt and the melted chocolate, whisking until they're completely combined. Add the rest of the dry ingredients; mix just until the last streak of flour is incorporated. Toss the reserved flour with the chopped chocolate chunks, then fold them into the batter until they're evenly distributed.

Pour the batter into the prepared pan, and bake the bread for 60 minutes, or until the loaf feels set on the outside and doesn't sink when you make an indentation in it with your finger. Remove the loaf from the oven, and allow it to cool in the pan for 30 minutes. Remove the bread to a cooling rack to cool completely to room temperature.

To make the chocolate buttercream, make the half batch of Russian Buttercream, then add the cocoa powder and the vanilla bean paste until they're incorporated.

Spread the buttercream evenly over the brownie bread. Refrigerate the bread for 20 minutes to set the frosting before slicing it.

This Chocolate Lover's Brownie Bread is best served at room temperature and stored, refrigerated, in an airtight container for up to a week.

YIELD: 10 SLICES

BROWNIE BREAD

½ cup (87 g) semisweet chocolate chips

1½ cups (180 g) all-purpose flour, spooned and leveled

½ cup (40 g) Dutch-process cocoa powder, spooned and leveled

¼ tsp baking soda

1 tsp baking powder

½ tsp salt

½ cup (113 g) unsalted butter, melted

2 large eggs, room temperature

1½ cups (300 g) granulated sugar

1 cup (227 g) Greek yogurt

½ cup (71 g) semisweet baking chocolate, roughly chopped

CHOCOLATE RUSSIAN BUTTERCREAM

½ batch of Russian Buttercream (page 18)

¼ cup (20 g) unsweetened cocoa powder, spooned and leveled

1 tsp vanilla bean paste or high-quality vanilla extract

WHITE CHOCOLATE PEACH DONUT SHORTCAKES

This is one of the last recipes I worked on. It's definitely one of my top five favorites! Strawberry shortcakes are cool and all, but peaches are my favorite fruit, and you can't ever go wrong with an old-fashioned cinnamon sugar donut. I replaced the whipped cream with the fluffiest White Chocolate Ermine Buttercream. I'm telling you; these babies will put any other shortcake to shame.

Begin by making the custard for the Ermine Buttercream at least a few hours before frosting the shortcakes, so it has time to cool.

For the donuts, preheat the oven to 350°F (177°C), and grease a donut pan. This recipe makes 18 donuts, but the batter can rest while you bake one pan at a time. Grease the pan between each batch.

In a small bowl, whisk together the flour, baking powder, baking soda, cinnamon, nutmeg and salt.

In a large bowl, whisk together the oil, granulated and brown sugars and eggs until they're fully combined. Add the vanilla and sour cream, mixing until they're fully incorporated. Fold in the dry ingredients just until the last streak of flour is incorporated.

Use a spoon or a piping bag to fill the donut molds about three-quarters full. Bake the donuts for about 9 minutes, or until an indentation made in them with your finger springs back. Allow them to cool in the pan for 5 minutes, then turn them onto a cooling rack.

For the Cinnamon Sugar Coating, whisk together the sugar, cinnamon and nutmeg in a shallow bowl. When all of the donuts are baked, use a pastry brush to brush melted butter onto a donut, then immediately toss the donut in the cinnamon sugar, coating it completely. Set it aside and repeat for the rest of the donuts.

(Continued)

WHITE CHOCOLATE ERMINE BUTTERCREAM

1 batch of Ermine Buttercream (page 17)

⅓ cup (58 g) white chocolate chips

1 tsp vanilla bean paste or high-quality vanilla extract

CINNAMON SUGAR DONUTS

2½ cups (300 g) all-purpose flour, spooned and leveled

½ tsp baking powder

½ tsp baking soda

1 tsp cinnamon

½ tsp nutmeg

½ tsp salt

½ cup (120 ml) canola oil

½ cup (100 g) granulated sugar

½ cup (95 g) packed brown sugar

2 large eggs, room temperature

1 tsp vanilla extract

1 cup (227 g) sour cream

CINNAMON SUGAR COATING

1 cup (200 g) granulated sugar

1 tsp cinnamon

¼ tsp nutmeg

2–3 tbsp (28–42 g) unsalted butter, melted

For the Peach Filling, in a medium bowl, toss the peaches with the sugar, cinnamon, nutmeg and salt until the peaches are evenly coated. Set the peaches aside to marinate.

For the white chocolate buttercream, melt the white chocolate chips in a small heatproof bowl in the microwave for 15-second intervals, stirring after each interval, until the chocolate is completely smooth, about 1 minute. Set aside the chocolate to cool. Finish making the Ermine Buttercream, then add the cooled chocolate and the vanilla bean paste, and mix until they're incorporated.

For serving, slice each of the donuts in half, like a bagel. Use a spoon or a piping bag to frost half of the donut halves. Top the frosting on each half with a few slices of peaches, then place another half of a donut on top. Refrigerate the donuts for 15 to 30 minutes to set the frosting.

These White Chocolate Peach Donut Shortcakes are best served at room temperature or slightly chilled. Store them in an airtight container in the fridge for 2 to 3 days.

PEACH FILLING
2 large peaches, peeled and thinly sliced

2 tbsp (28 g) packed brown sugar

¼ tsp cinnamon

⅛ tsp nutmeg

⅛ tsp salt

FROSTED

COOKIES & CREAM SWEET ROLLS

Cookies and cream rolls have been on my to-do list FOREVER! I can't believe I waited this long to make these sweet, chocolaty rolls, filled with crushed Oreo cookies and topped with a melty, Oreo-filling–infused Cream Cheese Frosting (page 19).

For the Chocolate Dough, grease a 9 x 13 x 2–inch (33 x 23 x 5–cm) baking sheet, and line it with parchment paper.

In a small bowl, stir the milk, yeast and 2 tablespoons (25 g) of the sugar until it's mostly combined, then set it aside to rest for 10 minutes. The milk should foam up on top.

Meanwhile, place the flour, the remaining 2 tablespoons (25 g) of the sugar, the cocoa powder and salt in the bowl of a stand mixer fitted with the hook attachment. Turn the mixer to low speed, add the egg and egg yolk, followed by the milk mixture and the butter. Once they're all combined, turn the mixer to medium-low speed and allow it to knead the dough for 10 to 15 minutes, until the dough begins to peel itself away from the sides of the bowl and form a ball around the hook attachment. If this doesn't happen, the dough is too sticky, so add 1 to 2 tablespoons (7 to 14 g) of flour and continue to knead until the dough comes together.

Push the dough to one side of the bowl, grease the open side and repeat with the other side. Cover the bowl with plastic wrap. Place the bowl in a warm environment, in the sunlight or on a stovetop warming zone, and allow it to proof until it's doubled in size, about 1 hour.

For the Oreo Filling, on a well-floured surface, use a rolling pin to roll the dough into an even rectangle about ¼ inch (6 mm) thick. Spread the butter evenly on the dough and top it with the sugar and crushed cookies.

Beginning at the short end, roll the dough as tightly as possible into a log. Grease a large knife, then cut the roll into 12 slices.

Place the rolls into the prepared pan, about 1 inch (2.5 cm) apart. Cover the pan, and place it in a warm environment. Proof the rolls for 30 to 60 minutes, until they look fluffy. Then, preheat the oven to 350°F (177°C). Bake the rolls for about 22 minutes, or until the edges of the rolls feel set but the centers still feel soft.

(Continued)

YIELD: 12 ROLLS

CHOCOLATE DOUGH

1 cup (240 ml) milk, warmed to 120°F (49°C)

2¼ tsp (7 g) active dry yeast

¼ cup (50 g) granulated sugar, divided

3 cups (360 g) all-purpose flour, spooned and leveled, plus more if needed

½ cup (40 g) Dutch-process cocoa powder, spooned and leveled

½ tsp salt

1 large egg, room temperature

1 large egg yolk, room temperature

½ cup (113 g) unsalted butter, softened

OREO FILLING

¼ cup (56 g) unsalted butter, softened

¼ cup (50 g) granulated sugar

12 chocolate sandwich cookies (I use Oreo), cream filling removed and reserved; cookies crushed

For the frosting, make the half batch of Cream Cheese Frosting. Add the reserved cream filling from the cookies, the cream and vanilla bean paste, and mix until they're fully incorporated.

Spread the frosting on top of the warm rolls.

These Cookies and Cream Rolls are best served fresh and warm. Store them in an airtight container at room temperature for up to 24 hours or refrigerated for up to a week.

TIP:

If you don't have a stand mixer, you can use your hands to combine the dough and to knead it. The dough is ready for proofing when you stretch it between your fingers and it's thin enough to see light through it without it ripping.

OREO CREAM CHEESE FROSTING

½ batch of Cream Cheese Frosting (page 19)

2 tbsp (30 ml) heavy whipping cream, cold

½ tsp vanilla bean paste or high-quality vanilla extract

CHAI-SPICED PEAR LOAF

Anyone else love chai spices as much as me? I knew this loaf was going to be good, but I was taken aback at how much I loved it. Get your spices out, pretend it's the holiday season and enjoy that fluffy spiced buttercream on top of your pear-infused loaf cake.

Begin by making the custard for the Ermine Buttercream at least a few hours before frosting the loaf, so it has time to cool. When you add the flour in the Ermine base recipe, also add the cinnamon, ginger, nutmeg, cardamom, cloves, allspice and pepper.

For the Pear Loaf, preheat the oven to 350°F (177°C). Grease a 9 x 5 x 3–inch (23 x 13 x 6–cm) loaf pan, and line it with parchment paper.

Place the pears on a paper towel, and cover them with another paper towel to soak up any excess liquid.

In a medium bowl, whisk together the flour, baking powder, salt, cinnamon, ginger, nutmeg, cardamom, cloves, allspice and pepper.

In a large bowl, whisk together the eggs, granulated and brown sugars and oil until they're well combined. Add the Greek yogurt, vanilla and the lemon zest, and mix until the mixture is smooth. Add the dry ingredients and mix just until the last streak of flour is combined.

Pour the batter into the prepared pan, and place the slices of pears into the batter, standing upright, in a line alternating right and left. Bake the loaf for 60 minutes, or until the center springs back when you press on it with your finger. Allow the loaf to cool in the pan for 30 minutes, then remove it and let it cool completely to room temperature.

Finish the Ermine Buttercream, then add the vanilla bean paste and beat just until it's fully incorporated.

Spread the frosting onto the loaf and dust it with cinnamon. Refrigerate the loaf for at least 20 minutes before slicing it.

This Chai-Spiced Pear Loaf is best served slightly chilled or at room temperature. Store it in an airtight container in the fridge for up to a week.

YIELD: 10 SLICES

CHAI SPICE ERMINE BUTTERCREAM
1 batch of Ermine Buttercream (page 17)

½ tsp cinnamon, plus more for dusting

¼ tsp ginger

¼ tsp nutmeg

¼ tsp cardamom

¼ tsp cloves

¼ tsp allspice

¼ tsp black pepper

½ tsp vanilla bean paste or high-quality vanilla extract

PEAR LOAF
2 medium Bosc pears, thinly sliced

1¾ cups (210 g) all-purpose flour, spooned and leveled

2½ tsp (12 g) baking powder

½ tsp salt

1½ tsp (3 g) cinnamon

½ tsp ginger

½ tsp nutmeg

½ tsp cardamom

½ tsp cloves

½ tsp allspice

¼ tsp black pepper

2 large eggs, room temperature

½ cup (100 g) granulated sugar

½ cup (95 g) packed brown sugar

½ cup (120 ml) canola oil

¾ cup (170 g) Greek yogurt

1 tsp vanilla extract

Zest of 1 small lemon

CHOCOLATE BRIOCHE DONUTS

There are donuts and there are brioche donuts. Brioche donuts are so incredibly fluffy that they melt in your mouth! Of course, they're tossed in sugar, and I filled these with a simple Chocolate Bavarian Cream. These donuts will require some patience, but they are so worth it!

Begin by making the custard for the Bavarian Cream at least a few hours before frosting the donuts, so it has time to cool.

For the dough, in a small bowl, mix the water, yeast and half of the sugar. Mix until it's mostly combined, and then let it rest for 10 minutes. The milk should foam up on top.

Meanwhile, place the flour, the remaining 1½ tablespoons (18 g) of sugar and the salt in the bowl of a stand mixer fitted with the hook attachment. Turn the mixer to low speed, add the eggs and egg yolks, followed by the milk mixture and the butter. Once they're all combined, turn the mixer to medium-low speed and allow it to knead the dough for 10 to 15 minutes, or until the dough begins to peel itself away from the sides of the bowl and forms a ball around the hook attachment. If this doesn't happen within the kneading time, the dough is too sticky; add 1 to 2 tablespoons (7 to 14 g) of flour and continue to knead until the dough comes together.

Push the dough to one side of the bowl, grease the open side, then repeat with the other side. Cover the bowl with plastic wrap. Place the bowl in a warm environment, in the sunlight or on a stovetop warming zone, and allow it to proof until it's doubled in size; this may take anywhere from 1 to 2 hours.

Line two baking sheets with parchment paper, and flour a work surface. Once the dough has doubled in size and is really fluffy, place it on the prepared work surface, and split it in half. Roll each half into a log, and cut each log into 10 chunks. Roll each chunk into a tight ball and place the chunks on the prepared baking sheets. Cover the baking sheets with plastic wrap, and place them in a warm environment to proof for 30 minutes, until they puff up slightly more.

(Continued)

CHOCOLATE BAVARIAN CREAM
½ batch of Bavarian Cream (page 22)

¼ cup (20 g) unsweetened cocoa powder, spooned and leveled

1 tsp vanilla bean paste or high-quality vanilla extract

DOUGH
1 cup (240 ml) water, warmed to 120°F (49°C)

2¼ tsp (7 g) active dry yeast

3 tbsp (36 g) granulated sugar, divided

4½ cups (540 g) all-purpose flour, spooned and leveled, plus more as needed

1 tsp salt

2 large eggs, room temperature

2 large egg yolks, room temperature

½ cup (113 g) unsalted butter, softened

Prepare for frying the donuts by lining two cooling racks with paper towels and spreading the sugar in a shallow bowl or pie tin.

Ten minutes before the donuts are done proofing, heat the oil in a large pot over high heat to about 360°F (182°C) on a candy thermometer, then lower the heat to medium. Use the thermometer to keep the oil within 10 degrees of 360°F (182°C). Depending on the size of your pot, place two to four donuts in the oil at a time, being sure to leave space around them. Fry the donuts on each side for 1 to 2 minutes, until they've browned, using a slotted spoon to flip them. If it is taking longer than 2 minutes to brown one side of the donut, increase the heat just a little. Work quickly, and avoid having an empty pot, so the oil doesn't burn. Set the fried donuts on the prepared racks.

While the next batch are frying and the donuts are still warm, toss them in sugar until they're evenly coated. Set them aside to finish cooling completely.

For the Chocolate Bavarian Cream, finish the Bavarian Cream, then add the cocoa powder and vanilla bean paste, and mix just until they're fully incorporated.

Use a knife to make a hole about halfway through the side of each donut. Use a piping bag to fill the holes with the Chocolate Bavarian Cream.

These Chocolate Brioche Donuts are best served at room temperature or slightly chilled. Store them in an airtight container in the fridge for two to three days.

TIP:
If you don't have a candy thermometer, heat the oil in a large pot over high heat until, when you put the end of a wooden spoon in the oil, the oil starts to bubble. If it's bubbling violently, lower the heat. The oil is within the right temperature range as long as it is bubbling around the donuts and not smoking, and the donuts brown within 1 to 2 minutes.

FOR FRYING
1–2 cups (200–400 g) granulated sugar, for tossing

4–6 cups (946 ml–1.4 L) canola oil

FROSTED

COOKIE BUTTER CINNAMON ROLLS

This is the third recipe in the book using cookie butter, so I think my obsession with it is no secret. Funny story: The first time I tasted cookie butter, I ate the whole jar (don't tell my husband). Now, I just sneak it into desserts, so the amount of cookie butter I go through seems more appropriate. With these cinnamon rolls, I developed a way to sneak cookie butter into breakfast. You can never go wrong with cinnamon rolls, but you also can't be more right to add cookie butter to them, especially in the form of melted frosting.

For the dough, grease a 9 x 13 x 2–inch (33 x 23 x 5–cm) baking pan, and line it with parchment paper.

In a small bowl, combine the milk, yeast and 2 tablespoons (25 g) of the granulated sugar until the ingredients are mostly combined, and then let the mixture rest for 10 minutes. The milk should foam up on top.

Meanwhile, place the flour, the remaining 2 tablespoons (25 g) of sugar and the salt in the bowl of a stand mixer fitted with the hook attachment. Turn the mixer to low speed, add the egg and egg yolk, followed by the milk mixture and the butter. Once they're all combined, turn the mixer to medium-low speed and allow it to knead the dough for 10 to 15 minutes, until it begins to peel itself away from the sides of the bowl and forms a ball around the hook attachment. If this doesn't happen, the dough is too sticky; add 1 to 2 tablespoons (7 to 14 g) of flour and continue to knead until the dough comes together.

Push the dough to one side of the bowl, grease the open side, then repeat with the opposite side. Cover the bowl with plastic wrap. Place the bowl in a warm environment, in the sunlight or on a stovetop warming zone, and allow it to proof until it's doubled in size, about 1 hour.

For the filling, combine the cookie butter and butter in a small bowl.

On a well-floured surface, use a rolling pin to roll the dough into a rectangle about ¼ inch (6 mm) thick. Spread the cookie butter mixture evenly on the dough, then sprinkle it with the cookies. Beginning at the short end, roll the dough as tightly as possible. Grease a large knife, then cut the roll into 12 slices.

(Continued)

DOUGH

1 cup (240 ml) milk, heated to 120°F (49°C)

2¼ tsp (7 g) active dry yeast

¼ cup (50 g) granulated sugar, divided

3½ cups (420 g) all-purpose flour, spooned and leveled, plus more as needed

½ tsp salt

1 large egg, room temperature

1 large egg yolk, room temperature

½ cup (113 g) unsalted butter, softened

COOKIE BUTTER FILLING

¾ cup (180 g) cookie butter (I use Lotus Biscoff)

½ cup (113 g) unsalted butter, melted

10 speculoos cookies (I use Lotus Biscoff)

COOKIE BUTTER CINNAMON ROLLS
(Continued)

Place the rolls into the prepared pan, about 1 inch (2.5 cm) apart. Cover the pan, and place it in a warm environment for the rolls to proof for 30 to 60 minutes, until they look fluffy.

Preheat the oven to 350°F (177°C), and bake the rolls for 20 to 25 minutes, just until the dough is a golden color.

Make the half batch of American Buttercream, add the cookie butter and cream, and mix until they're fully incorporated.

Spread the frosting on top of the warm cinnamon rolls, and sprinkle the cookies on the frosting.

These Cookie Butter Cinnamon Rolls are best served fresh and warm. Store, in an airtight container, at room temperature for up to 24 hours, or refrigerated for up to a week.

TIP:
If you don't have a stand mixer, you can use your hands to combine the dough and to knead it. The dough is ready for proofing when you stretch it between your fingers and it's thin enough to see light through it without it ripping.

COOKIE BUTTER AMERICAN FROSTING
½ batch of American Buttercream (page 11)

¼ cup (56 g) cookie butter (I use Lotus Biscoff)

2 tbsp (30 ml) heavy whipping cream, cold

TOPPING
2–3 speculoos cookies (I use Lotus Biscoff), crushed

BIRTHDAY CAKE **LOAF**

There is no better way to start your birthday than with a breakfast version of birthday cake! You know it's never a bad day if it starts with sprinkles. I frosted this baby with a creamy Chocolate American Meringue Buttercream, basically turning the classic American birthday cake into your new favorite breakfast.

For the birthday loaf, preheat the oven to 350°F (177°C). Grease a 9 x 5 x 3–inch (23 x 13 x 6–cm) loaf pan with baking spray, and line it with parchment paper.

In a medium bowl, whisk together the flour, baking powder and salt.

In the bowl of a stand mixer fitted with the whisk attachment, beat the butter and sugar together, on medium speed, until they're light and fluffy. This should take 2 to 3 minutes. Then add the eggs, one at a time, beating well after each addition for about 30 seconds. Make sure to scrape the sides and bottom of the bowl as needed. Add the sour cream, vanilla and artificial vanilla, and mix just until they're combined.

With the mixer at low speed, add half of the dry ingredients to the mixture, followed by the milk and then the second half of the dry ingredients. Beat the mixture on medium speed, just until the flour is fully incorporated, making sure to scrape the flour from the sides of the bowl. Add the sprinkles, and mix just until they're evenly distributed.

Pour the batter into the prepared pan, and bake the loaf for 65 to 70 minutes, until an indentation made in the cake with your finger springs back. Remove the loaf from the pan, and allow it to cool completely.

Next, make the Chocolate American Meringue Buttercream. Melt the chocolate chips, in a small heatproof bowl, in the microwave on 20-second intervals, stirring after each addition, until the chocolate is completely smooth, 1 to 2 minutes. Set aside the chocolate to cool to room temperature. Make the half batch of American Meringue Buttercream, then add the cooled chocolate, cocoa powder and vanilla bean paste, mixing until they're completely incorporated.

Spread the buttercream over the cooled loaf and top it with the sprinkles. Refrigerate the loaf for about 20 minutes before slicing it.

This Birthday Cake Loaf is best served at room temperature and stored, refrigerated, in an airtight container for up to a week.

YIELD: 10 SLICES

SPRINKLE VANILLA LOAF
2¼ cups (270 g) all-purpose flour, spooned and leveled

2½ tsp (12 g) baking powder

½ tsp salt

¾ cup (170 g) unsalted butter, room temperature

1½ cups (300 g) granulated sugar

3 large eggs, room temperature

½ cup (113 g) sour cream

1 tsp vanilla extract

1 tsp artificial vanilla extract

½ cup (120 ml) milk, room temperature

⅓ cup (50 g) rainbow sequin sprinkles

CHOCOLATE AMERICAN MERINGUE BUTTERCREAM
¼ cup (44 g) dark chocolate chips

½ batch of American Meringue Buttercream (page 12)

¼ cup (20 g) unsweetened cocoa powder, spooned and leveled

½ tsp vanilla bean paste

TOPPING
2 tbsp (20 g) rainbow sequin sprinkles

TASTY TARTS

This chapter is so great because it really shows you how to use frosting outside of the box. There's more to frosting than just icing a cake or a cupcake or sandwiching it between cookies. Just by cutting back on the sugar a little, I was able to use Cream Cheese Frosting (page 19) as a filling for the No-Bake Peanut Butter Cheesecake (page 174). I also used Chocolate Ganache (page 21) as a tart filling for the White Chocolate Strawberry Tart (page 173) and Bavarian Cream (page 22) as a filling for the Chocolate Hazelnut Silk Pie (page 181).

Use this chapter to experiment with the frostings, and build off my recipes to create your own. Instead of a No-Bake Peanut Butter Cheesecake (page 174), try a no-bake cookie butter cheesecake. Or, instead of a Chocolate Hazelnut Silk Pie (page 181), try a white chocolate silk pie. I definitely recommend making the original recipe first, so you have something to compare it to, but don't be afraid to experiment. My absolute favorite thing about baking is the creativity of trying new things.

Just like frosting, tarts are pretty difficult to define. Most define a tart as an open pastry containing some sort of filling. So, in this chapter you'll find recipes that are built around a crust, a filling and, of course, a frosting. All of these recipes are baked in a round tart pan, rectangular tart pan or a pie dish. The pans are pretty interchangeable, so these treats can be baked in whatever pans you have available.

For this chapter, it's important to remember that crusts need chill time, fillings need chill time and frostings need chill time, so you're going to need some serious chill time for yourself. Don't be tempted to skip these necessary steps! I promise you'll be much happier with your results, because good things are always worth waiting for.

WHITE CHOCOLATE STRAWBERRY TART

Get ready to have the best White Chocolate Strawberry Tart of your life! This chocolate crust is filled with a thick White Chocolate Ganache (page 21), sandwiched around a layer of fresh, sweet strawberries and topped with a drizzle of dark chocolate.

For the filling, place the strawberries on a paper towel and cover them with another sheet of paper towel, to soak up any excess liquid. Allowing the strawberries to dry out for several hours will prevent them from leaking inside the tart.

For the Chocolate Crust, lightly grease a 14 x 4 x 1–inch (36 x 10 x 2.5–cm) tart pan. In a medium bowl, whisk together the flour, sugar, cocoa powder and salt.

In a large bowl, combine the butter and vanilla. Fold the dry ingredients into the butter mixture just until the last streak of flour is combined. Firmly press the crust onto the bottom and sides of the tart pan. Freeze the crust for 20 minutes, and preheat the oven to 350°F (177°C).

Place a sheet of parchment paper on top of the crust, then top the paper with pie weights (or rice). Bake the crust for 15 minutes, or until the edges feel set. Remove the crust from the oven, and remove the parchment paper and pie weights. Bake the crust for 7 minutes, or until the center is dried and the edges are set. Allow the crust to cool completely to room temperature.

Continue with the filling, making two batches of Thick White Chocolate Ganache. Pour half of the ganache on the bottom of the crust, and refrigerate the tart until the ganache is firm, about 20 minutes. Spread the strawberries evenly on the chilled white chocolate, and pour the rest of the ganache over the strawberries; you may need to reheat the chocolate if it has cooled too much to spread. Refrigerate the tart for at least a couple of hours, until the white chocolate feels firm.

For the topping, in a small bowl, melt the chocolate with the coconut oil in the microwave for 20-second intervals, stirring after each interval, until it's smooth, 1 to 2 minutes. Use a spoon to drizzle the chocolate over the chilled white chocolate. Refrigerate the tart for 5 to 10 minutes, until the chocolate is set, then cut into slices.

This White Chocolate Strawberry Tart is best served slightly chilled. Store it in an airtight container in the fridge for two to three days.

YIELD: 12 SLICES

WHITE CHOCOLATE FILLING
12 medium strawberries, thinly sliced

2 batches of Thick White Chocolate Ganache (page 21)

CHOCOLATE CRUST
1 cup (120 g) all-purpose flour, spooned and leveled

¼ cup (50 g) granulated sugar

¼ cup (20 g) Dutch-process cocoa powder, spooned and leveled

¼ tsp salt

½ cup (113 g) unsalted butter, melted

1 tsp vanilla extract

TOPPING
¼ cup (44 g) dark chocolate chips

2 tsp (10 g) coconut oil

NO-BAKE PEANUT BUTTER CHEESECAKE

This amazing no-bake cheesecake is so fun! It shows you how to make a cheesecake filling from a frosting recipe. I took my Cream Cheese Frosting (page 19) recipe, halved the sugar, added peanut butter and voila! With an easy graham cracker crust and a gorgeous toasted meringue on top, this cheesecake is sure to impress.

For the crust, place the graham crackers in a food processor and pulse until they're completely crushed, 1 to 2 minutes. Add the butter, and pulse for a few seconds, until the butter is evenly distributed. Pour the crust into a 9-inch (23-cm) pie pan and press it firmly against the bottom and sides of the pan. Freeze the crust for at least 20 minutes.

For the filling, make the batch of Cream Cheese Frosting. Add the peanut butter, cream, vanilla bean paste and cinnamon; beat the mixture, at full speed, for 2 minutes. Spread the peanut butter—cream cheese filling over the crust, and refrigerate the tart for at least 2 hours, until the filling is firm.

Make the Meringue Frosting, add the vanilla bean paste and the cinnamon and beat the meringue until they're fully incorporated. Use a spoon or an offset spatula to spread the meringue on the cheesecake, and use a kitchen torch or a lighter to toast the meringue.

Refrigerate the cheesecake for at least 30 minutes to set, then slice it.

This No-Bake Peanut Butter Cheesecake is best served slightly chilled. Store it in an airtight container in the fridge for up to a week.

GRAHAM CRACKER CRUST

1 sleeve (300 g) honey graham crackers

¼ cup (56 g) unsalted butter, melted

PEANUT BUTTER CHEESECAKE FILLING

1 batch of Cream Cheese Frosting (page 19), use only half of the powdered sugar

½ cup (115 g) creamy peanut butter (I use Jif)

2 tbsp (30 ml) heavy whipping cream, cold

1 tsp vanilla bean paste or high-quality vanilla extract

¼ tsp cinnamon

MERINGUE FROSTING

1 batch of Meringue Frosting (page 20)

1 tsp vanilla bean paste or high-quality vanilla extract

½ tsp cinnamon

LEMON POPPY SEED BLONDIE PIE

Is a frosted blondie baked in a pie dish still considered a blondie, or does being baked in a pie dish make it a pie? I'm going to go with, "I don't care," because this Lemon Poppy Seed Blondie Pie is a little slice of heaven. It's got chewy vanilla blondie, a delicious homemade lemon curd and the best fluffy lemon cream, studded with tiny poppy seeds.

To make the lemon curd, combine the lemon zest, lemon juice, egg, egg yolk, sugar, butter, salt and vanilla bean paste in a medium saucepan over medium-low heat. Whisk the mixture continuously for 5 to 10 minutes, until the curd begins to thicken and coat the back of a spoon. Remove the curd from the heat and pour it into a heatproof bowl. Cover the surface with plastic wrap, and cool the curd completely to room temperature, about 2 hours. Once it's cooled, refrigerate it.

While cooling the lemon curd, make the custard for the Diplomat Cream, so it also has time to cool for a few hours.

For the blondie, preheat the oven to 350°F (177°C). Grease a 9-inch (23-cm) pie dish, and line it with parchment paper.

In a medium bowl, whisk together the butter and granulated and brown sugars. Add the egg and vanilla, and mix until they're fully combined. Fold in the flour and salt just until the last streak of flour is incorporated. Spread the blondie batter evenly in the prepared pan.

Bake the blondie for 30 minutes, or until the edges are set but the center is still soft. Remove the blondie from the oven, and allow it to cool completely to room temperature, about 2 hours. Spread half of the chilled lemon curd on top of the blondies, and refrigerate the tart for 20 minutes.

Finish the Diplomat Cream, then add the remaining half of the lemon curd, the vanilla bean paste and the poppy seeds, mixing just until they're incorporated. Spread the cream on top of the lemon curd in the tart, and refrigerate the tart for at least 1 hour to set.

Top the tart with the lemon slices, lemon zest and poppy seeds, if using, and cut into slices. Lemon Poppy Seed Blondie Pie is best served slightly chilled. Store it in an airtight container in the fridge for up to a week.

YIELD: 10 SLICES

LEMON CURD
Zest of 1 large lemon

¼ cup (60 ml) freshly squeezed lemon juice

1 large egg

1 large egg yolk

¼ cup (50 g) granulated sugar

3 tbsp (42 g) unsalted butter, softened

⅛ tsp salt

½ tsp vanilla bean paste or high-quality vanilla extract

LEMON POPPY SEED DIPLOMAT CREAM
1 batch of Diplomat Cream (page 23)

½ tsp vanilla bean paste or high-quality vanilla extract

1 tbsp (9 g) poppy seeds

BLONDIE
½ cup (113 g) unsalted butter, melted

¼ cup (50 g) granulated sugar

½ cup (95 g) packed brown sugar

1 large egg, room temperature

1 tsp vanilla extract

1 cup (120 g) all-purpose flour, spooned and leveled

¼ tsp salt

TOPPING
Lemon slices, lemon zest and poppy seeds, optional

COOKIE MOCHA TART

FRIENDS! When I was working on this recipe, I was doing a diet challenge and this bad boy got me good. I mean I can't blame him, I combined three of the most addicting foods—cookies, chocolate and coffee—to create him. The espresso meringue is to die for; however, it does compromise the structure of the meringue, because you're adding liquid, not powder, so the meringue will definitely be a little softer than usual.

For the cookie crust, lightly grease a 14 x 4 x 1–inch (36 x 10 x 2.5–cm) tart pan.

In a medium bowl, whisk together the flour, baking soda and salt.

In a large bowl, whisk together the butter with the brown and granulated sugars, then add the egg and vanilla. Mix until the mixture is completely combined. Fold in the dry ingredients just until the last streak of flour is incorporated. Fold in the chocolate chips until they're evenly distributed.

Press the cookie dough onto the bottom and up the sides of the tart pan, and freeze it for 30 minutes.

Preheat the oven to 350°F (177°C). Place a piece of parchment paper on the crust, and top the paper with pie weights (or rice). Bake the crust for 15 minutes, until the edges are golden brown. Remove the pie weights and parchment paper, and bake for 5 minutes, until the center is golden brown and feels soft but not set. Cool the crust for at least 30 minutes.

For the filling, make the Thin Milk Chocolate Ganache, and pour it on top of the cooled cookie crust. Refrigerate or freeze the tart until it's chilled and the chocolate sets, at least 2 hours.

Make the Meringue Frosting when the chocolate in the tart is set. Add the espresso and vanilla bean paste, mixing just until they're combined. Spread the espresso meringue on top of the chilled chocolate ganache. Use a kitchen torch or a lighter to toast the meringue.

Refrigerate the tart for about 30 minutes to set, then cut it into slices.

This Cookie Mocha Tart is best served cold or slightly chilled. Store it in an airtight container in the fridge for two to three days.

YIELD: 12 SLICES

CHOCOLATE CHIP COOKIE CRUST
1 cup (120 g) all-purpose flour, spooned and leveled

¼ tsp baking soda

½ tsp salt

½ cup (113 g) unsalted butter, melted

¼ cup (47 g) packed brown sugar

¼ cup (50 g) granulated sugar

1 large egg, room temperature

1 tsp vanilla extract

½ cup (87 g) semisweet chocolate chips

CHOCOLATE GANACHE FILLING
1½ batches of Thin Milk Chocolate Ganache (page 21)

ESPRESSO MERINGUE FROSTING
1 batch of Meringue Frosting (page 20)

2 tbsp (30 ml) brewed espresso, chilled

½ tsp vanilla bean paste or high-quality vanilla extract

CHOCOLATE HAZELNUT
SILK PIE

Chocolate silk pies are one of the best inventions of mankind; can I get an amen?! There are so many methods of making silk pie, and I don't think any of them are bad. As you already know, Bavarian Cream (page 22) can be a dessert on its own. But, it's so much better when you add chocolate hazelnut spread, put it on top of an Oreo crust and top it with fresh whipped cream. This is my easy imitation of a chocolate silk pie.

Begin by making the custard for the Bavarian Cream at least a few hours before assembling the cake, so it has time to cool.

For the Oreo Crust, place the chocolate sandwich cookies in a food processor, and pulse until they're completely crushed, 1 to 2 minutes. Add the butter and pulse for a few seconds, until the butter is evenly distributed.

In a 9-inch (23-cm) tart pan, press the crust firmly against the bottom and sides of the pan. Freeze the crust for at least 20 minutes.

Finish the Bavarian Cream, then add the chocolate hazelnut spread, cocoa powder and vanilla bean paste; mix just until they're fully incorporated. Spread the Chocolate Hazelnut Bavarian Cream on top of the crust, and refrigerate it for at least 2 hours to set.

Just before serving the tart, make the whipped topping. With an electric mixer, at full speed, beat the cream with the powdered sugar and vanilla bean paste until stiff peaks form. Spread it on top of the Bavarian Cream, and cut the tart into slices.

This Chocolate Hazelnut Silk Pie is best served at room temperature or slightly chilled. Store it in an airtight container in the fridge for up to a week.

YIELD: 10 SLICES

CHOCOLATE HAZELNUT BAVARIAN CREAM
½ batch of Bavarian Cream (page 22)

¼ cup (73 g) chocolate hazelnut spread (I use Nutella)

¼ cup (20 g) cocoa powder, spooned and leveled

½ tsp vanilla bean paste or high-quality vanilla extract

OREO CRUST
25 (300 g) chocolate sandwich cookies (I use Oreo)

¼ cup (56 g) unsalted butter, melted

WHIPPED TOPPING
1 cup (240 ml) heavy whipping cream, cold

2 tbsp (16 g) powdered sugar, spooned and leveled

½ tsp vanilla bean paste or high-quality vanilla extract

BROWN SUGAR S'MORES CHEESECAKE

S'mores is my all-time favorite flavor, and I dream of making a s'mores version of everything. My blog features a s'mores layer cake, donuts, sweet rolls and sugar cookies: basically everything. But I saved this beautiful s'mores cheesecake just for you!

For the crust, place a large pan halfway full of water on the bottom rack of the oven, and preheat the oven to 350°F (177°C). Grease a 10-inch (25-cm) springform pan.

Place the graham crackers in a food processor and pulse until they're completely crushed, 1 to 2 minutes. Add the brown sugar, salt, cinnamon and butter, and pulse until they're evenly distributed. Firmly press the crust into the prepared pan, coming halfway up the sides, then freeze it while you make the cheesecake.

For the filling, in a stand mixer fitted with a paddle attachment, cream the cream cheese and brown sugar. Do this at medium-low speed, just until they're creamy and fully combined, scraping down the sides of the bowl as needed. Add the sour cream, vanilla bean paste, cornstarch and salt, and mix just until the batter is smooth. Add the eggs, followed by the egg yolks, mixing at low speed, just until the batter is completely smooth.

Pour the cheesecake batter over the crust, and bake the cheesecake for 75 minutes, until the edges are set and the center is still jiggly. Turn off the oven, crack open the door and let the cheesecake rest for 30 minutes. Remove the cheesecake from the oven, allow it to cool to room temperature, then refrigerate it for 4 hours or up to overnight.

Make one batch of Thin Milk Chocolate Ganache, and pour it over the chilled cheesecake.

Refrigerate the cheesecake while you make the batch of Meringue Frosting, using brown sugar instead of granulated sugar. Add the vanilla bean paste, and beat the meringue until it's fully incorporated.

Use a spoon or an offset spatula to spread the meringue on top of the chilled ganache. Use a kitchen torch or a lighter to toast the meringue, then cut the cheesecake into slices.

This Brown Sugar S'mores Cheesecake is best served slightly chilled. Store it in an airtight container in the fridge for up to a week.

YIELD: 10 SLICES

CRUST
2 sleeves (600 g) honey graham crackers

1 tbsp (12 g) packed brown sugar

¼ tsp salt

¼ tsp cinnamon

½ cup (113 g) unsalted butter, melted

CHEESECAKE FILLING
32 oz (907 g) cream cheese, room temperature

1½ cups (285 g) packed brown sugar

1½ cups (340 g) sour cream, room temperature

1 tbsp (13 g) vanilla bean paste or high-quality vanilla extract

2 tbsp (16 g) cornstarch

¼ tsp salt

3 large eggs, room temperature

2 large egg yolks, room temperature

CHOCOLATE GANACHE
1 batch of Thin Milk Chocolate Ganache (page 21)

MERINGUE
1 batch of Meringue Frosting (page 20), use brown sugar instead of granulated sugar

1 tsp vanilla bean paste or high-quality vanilla extract

BROWN BUTTER VANILLA FRUIT TART

I'm not going to lie . . . I almost didn't eat a slice of this tart because it turned out so pretty. Keyword: almost. This is definitely my favorite recipe in this chapter; as each bite was perfect. And, when you get a taste of the peach in your bite, it is NEXT LEVEL. So, go ahead, judge this book by its cover, because she tastes as beautiful as she looks.

To brown the butter, place it in a small saucepan over medium heat and allow it to cook for about 10 minutes. Stir frequently until it begins to foam, then stir continuously. Soon after it begins to foam, you will see the milk solids browning and settling toward the bottom of the pan. The smell will also begin to change to a nutty aroma. When the butter turns a light amber color, remove it from the heat and pour it into a large heatproof mixing bowl. Allow it to cool until it's no longer piping hot, up to 30 minutes, before using it.

For the crust, lightly grease a 9-inch (23-cm) tart pan. In a medium bowl, whisk together the flour, sugar and salt. Add the vanilla to the cooled brown butter, then fold in the dry ingredients, just until the last streak of flour is combined.

Firmly press the crust onto the bottom and sides of the tart pan. Freeze the crust for 20 minutes while the oven is preheating to 350°F (177°C).

Place a sheet of parchment paper on top of the crust; top the paper with pie weights (or rice). Bake the crust for 15 minutes, until the edges are golden brown, then remove it from the oven and remove the parchment paper and pie weights. Bake the crust for 7 minutes, or until the center dries and is golden brown. Allow the crust to cool to room temperature.

Place the egg yolks, sugar and cornstarch in a small bowl, and whisk them until the eggs turn pale yellow, 1 to 2 minutes. Set aside the mixture. In a medium saucepan over medium-low heat, bring the milk to a simmer, stirring frequently. Once the milk is simmering, SLOWLY pour half of the milk over the eggs, while whisking the egg mixture continuously, to temper the eggs. Then, pour the whole mixture back into the pot with the remaining half of the milk. Stir it continuously over medium-low heat, for about 10 minutes. Once the custard begins to thicken and you see the first bubble pop, whisk the custard for 1 minute, then remove it from the heat. Stir in the butter, vanilla bean paste and salt, and pour the custard over the cooled crust. Refrigerate the tart until the custard is firm, at least 3 hours.

(Continued)

BROWN BUTTER
½ cup (113 g) unsalted butter

BROWN BUTTER CRUST
1 cup (120 g) all-purpose flour, spooned and leveled

¼ cup (50 g) granulated sugar

¼ tsp salt

1 tsp vanilla extract

VANILLA CUSTARD FILLING
8 egg yolks

¾ cup (150 g) granulated sugar

3 tbsp (24 g) cornstarch

1 cup (240 ml) whole milk

1 cup (227 g) unsalted butter, softened

2 tsp (8 g) vanilla bean paste or high-quality vanilla extract

⅛ tsp salt

BROWN BUTTER VANILLA FRUIT TART
(Continued)

For the topping, slice the peach and arrange the slices on a paper towel. Cover them with another paper towel to soak up some of the juice.

Make the half batch of Meringue Frosting, add the vanilla bean paste and mix just until it's incorporated.

Place the sliced peach, strawberries, cherries and blackberries on top of the chilled custard. Use a piping bag to pipe the frosting around the fruit. Use a kitchen torch or a lighter to toast the meringue, before cutting into slices.

This Brown Butter Vanilla Fruit Tart is best served slightly chilled. Store it in an airtight container in the fridge for three to four days.

VANILLA BEAN MERINGUE FROSTING
½ batch of Meringue Frosting (page 20)

1 tsp vanilla bean paste or high-quality vanilla extract

TOPPINGS
1 peach, sliced

2 strawberries

4 cherries

5 blackberries

ACKNOWLEDGMENTS

First, I thank God for every opportunity, every open and closed door and every broken road that got me here today. Thank you for giving me a way to combine science and art, for the ability to create beauty and for a simple way to put a smile on people's faces.

Narcis, thank you for supporting me and for being patient with me during this time. You're unapologetically honest about my recipes, photography and attitude; thank you for being my No. 1 fan and my biggest cheerleader. I love you, Musca.

Beckham, thank you for loving me more than Mara, even though I let you cry at my feet and she is willing to do anything for your love. Thanks for being the cutest kid on the planet #bias. I love you, Bobalicious.

Mom, thank you for all the recipes I stole from you, and for being the hardest worker I know. Thank you for answering my FaceTime calls 100 times a day and for babysitting Beckham. Dad, thank you for always pushing us to reach our highest potential in whatever we do and for being the best taste-tester.

Mars and Cars, thank you for absorbing most of my attitude and frustrations, so no one else has to endure them. Mara, I'm so glad you didn't like your other jobs and you saw potential in me and Baran Bakery. In case I didn't already tell you, you're the WORST taste-tester: Not everything I make is perfect, but I appreciate the encouragement. Carmen, thanks for making me laugh even when I don't want to. You're the second worst taste-tester, saying it's gross and then eating the whole thing isn't very helpful . . . I'm glad you came to your senses and realized that sugar is delicious.

To all the rest of my taste-testers, thank you for sacrificing some of your precious calories! Diana, Brendan, Carmen's coworkers, Dad's coworkers, Narcis's coworkers, playdate friends, Summit Church, Pastor Mike and family, and all of you wonderful people who came to pick up treats: Thank you, thank you, thank you!

Jenna Fagan and the rest of the Page Street Publishing team: Thank you for seeing something in me and for being patient with me throughout this process. Thank you for this dream come true and for putting together a beautiful book.

Sarah Crawford, thank you for sharing your wealth of knowledge. You showed me what's possible, inspired me to pursue my dream and you taught me how to turn my hobby into a career. Also, thanks for the best macaron base recipe!

To all my Baran Bakery friends, you made this dream possible for me. Thank you for making my recipes, following along on this journey and for being so supportive and encouraging.

ABOUT THE AUTHOR

BERNICE BARAN is the creator of Baran Bakery, a food blog focused mainly on sweets and baked goods, with a little dash of life and something savory. Butter and sugar run through her veins, because she grew up with a baker as a mom.

A self-taught baker, Bernice started Baran Bakery as a creative outlet after college. She began with her mom's Romanian and Hungarian pastries, then moved on to experimenting with American and French pastries before diving into the life of frosting. She currently lives among the Great Lakes with her husband, baby boy and their huge Romanian family.

INDEX